I KNOW

ELEVATE YOUR MINDSET

YOU'RE

TO RELEASE STRESS

IN THERE

AND UNLOCK YOUR TRUE POTENTIAL

SOMEWHERE

AMAL GRAMMAS

To Jimmy, Zoe & Yianni

CONTENTS

INTRODUCTION

I'm a leadership coach who works with leaders from all walks of life. My clients are amazing people who are motivated to continually grow and improve. They all have a few things in common: they want to make a positive impact on others, they want to achieve financial success, and they want to feel less stress and more peace. They have each done the tough work to identify the emotional patterns that have caused them pain and limited their positive influence on others.

Like my clients, I had blind spots and behavioral patterns that limited me. For most of my life, I pretended I was perfect. I pretended I was happy when what I was really feeling was far from it. I felt insecure, stressed out, and unfulfilled, and because of those feelings I lashed out. I wasn't fun to be around, and I lost my temper a lot more often than I would like to admit. I had a constant uneasy feeling, a low-grade anxiety that never really went away, and a heavy feeling in my chest. I wanted nothing more than to change the way I was feeling and acting, but I didn't know how. I tried so many things to make myself feel better: shopping, binging on Netflix, yoga, antidepressants, therapy, lots of wine, trips with friends, work, work, and more work. Nothing helped so I just kept pushing myself forward.

Then a few things happened that forced me to take a closer look at what wasn't working in my life: I blacked out briefly while driving on the highway; my mother died; I got fired. With each event, I made progress toward positive change, but it wasn't until the last one that I made profound changes by getting honest with myself at depths I'd never reached before. I finally got real. Real enough to ask myself the following questions: *What really mattered to me? How could I lead myself at my best? What needed to change for me to feel happy?* Before that, I didn't dare ask myself those questions because I was scared to face the answers.

Lead Yourself First

This is not your typical leadership book because it has more to do with leading yourself than leading others. When you lead yourself first, you improve self-confidence, people gravitate toward you, and you have more positive influence over them.

In this book I'll guide you to do some inner work to identify the things from your past that might be subconsciously blocking you from feeling your best. You'll take a hard look at how you've been living your life, and you'll get honest with yourself about what needs to change. Then, you'll learn how to create those changes by making small, incremental shifts every day. My goal is for you to feel inspired and energized by what you do so you can emerge as a leader in your own life and inspire others to be their best.

I'll be sharing ideas, stories, and principles that will help you understand and prepare for the exercises you'll complete throughout the book. In those exercises, I'll challenge you to take specific actions in your daily life that will help you lock in and implement what you've learned.

I start with my story because I've found that many people are going through what I went through, at least on some level. I may have reacted more aggressively to situations than you would have, but the lessons I learned from facing my fears and limitations are universal.

I am not a psychologist, or a medical doctor. I am a leadership coach. This book is intended for people who are motivated to continually improve. This is a book about real people, what they've gone through, and how they made profound changes in their lives. These are real stories, my own and my clients'. Names have been changed to respect privacy.

Note: If you believe you are suffering from a psychological or medical condition, please seek help from a qualified health professional.

CHAPTER 1

AN UNSUSTAINABLE LIFE

Our past gets in the way of our present more often than we realize. Most of us think we're good at hiding our baggage—but we carry it with us everywhere we go, even at work.

I worked in medical device sales for years. I started a sales job when I was six months pregnant, and I won Rookie of the Year and Rep of the Year. It was a tough selling environment, but I was a tough person, and I did well. I made great money, and I talked myself into believing that the more money I made, the happier I would be. But I was miserable for most of those years. I felt stressed out and exhausted all the time. Looking back, it makes sense: I was working so hard to portray perfection that I had no energy left over. Instead of dealing with those feelings, I dug deeper and worked harder, pushing my body and mind beyond their limits. Deep down I knew the way I was living wasn't sustainable, but I talked myself into believing that I could handle anything that came my way.

Until I couldn't. One morning, when I was rushing to a client meeting, I blacked out briefly while driving on the highway. I had been having heart palpitations for weeks, but I kept telling myself I was fine. I'd pushed myself so hard that I risked hurting myself, or other people. That moment scared me enough to make me realize something in my life had to change, so I made an appointment with a cardiologist, then I found a life coach.

Not long after blacking out at the wheel, my mom passed away. In the weeks and months that followed, I spiraled into a deep depression. I had reached a critical point, one that required something I hadn't been particularly good at: self-examination. I realized I was angry and continually frustrated. It took me longer to realize that those feelings came from something much deeper. There was a part of me that didn't feel good enough, and because of that, I felt sad and ashamed. I felt like a victim of circumstances, as if I had no control over what happened in my life and that, because of other people, my life wasn't going the way I wanted. I had a negative mindset. It had taken something big, like losing my mom, to notice that the to-do list wasn't enough to compensate for those problems. My life was out of balance.

I'd like to tell you that change happened quickly, that I tackled all my issues with speed and grace. But that's definitely not how it happened. There was so much in my life that needed changing, I didn't know where to start.

- I wanted to connect more with my kids, to have a more emotionally intimate relationship with my husband, to exercise more, and to sleep better.

- I didn't want to work in corporate America anymore, and I was sick and tired of selling products I wasn't passionate about.

- I wanted to make a real difference in people's lives, to do something meaningful.

- I wanted to feel lighthearted and calm instead of continually anxious, but I was too scared to make any big, lasting changes.

So, I took baby steps. I got a different sales job and convinced myself it would be the thing that brought me everything I was looking for. I thought changing my job would make me happy, but I learned that your issues follow you wherever you go.

Getting Fired

My new job didn't last long. I got fired for talking about using a product I was selling for a procedure it wasn't approved for. I told myself that everyone did what I was doing, and since the product would be used in a cosmetic procedure, no one would get hurt so it wasn't a big deal. Those were rationalizations.

I had always prided myself on my ability to get things done, and done right, so this was a big blow to my ego. I felt ashamed and embarrassed. Accountability didn't come naturally to me, because on some level, I thought the rules didn't apply to me. Getting fired was just what I needed to wake up and realize I was no different than anyone else, and that the way I was living was hurting me and hurting people around me.

Learning to Be Accountable

Although I had started working with a coach before getting fired, I had approached the coaching process the same way I had been approaching my life, by checking the boxes and going through the motions. I tell my clients I wasn't easy to coach at first because I was scared to get vulnerable, to be honest with myself, and let go of my ego. This experience pushed me to finally look at the traits that were limiting me, and the wounds that drove them. It was difficult but once I had made the commitment to changing my life, there was no turning back. My inner transformation was so profound that I became obsessed with the process of coaching. I spent six years studying with several coaching programs, including Robbins-Madanes Training, then I started my own business.

I began a new career helping people identify and overcome the obstacles that keep them from feeling fulfilled and reaching their true potential as leaders, and as human beings. The training was intense, but I learned to truly connect with people, let go of my ego, and lead from my heart. I doubted myself often, and there were times when we could barely pay our bills. But not having another choice gave me the kick in the butt I needed to keep going.

You may have an area of your life you want to change, too. If you feel nervous about it, that's completely natural. It's not easy, and it takes faith, tenacity, and a little bit of humility. Usually, people must reach the point where they can't live the way they've been living for even one more day before they can entertain the thought of transforming their lives. Let's hold off on worrying about that for now and think about smaller, more manageable changes that will motivate and energize you to build momentum. You will have plenty of time later in this process to make a thoughtful transition plan if that's what you need. For now, start to think about where you could be more accountable.

EXERCISE: Accountability

Accountability begins with getting honest with yourself about what you want and why you want it. Sometimes people don't hold themselves or others accountable because they're not clear about what they really want, or because they're avoiding something.

My definition of accountability is:

1. Knowing what you want

2. Being crystal clear with yourself and others about why you want it

3. Doing what you say you will do to get it done

Answer the questions below without thinking too much. Write down the first thing that comes to your mind. (That's your subconscious talking, and it always tells you the truth.)

1. What do you want? (What is the one thing that *must* happen in your life in the next twelve months?)

2. Why do you want it? (Why is it a must?)

CHAPTER 2

YOU ARE READY FOR CHANGE

Now you know what you want and why you want it. The next step is to gain more clarity about what you may need to change to make your goal a reality.

Leadership coaching requires self-examination, it forces you to get honest with yourself about what isn't working in your life. It's not easy and that's why so many people don't reach their full potential—their motivation isn't strong enough to confront the obstacles and challenges that arise. That could be because they're not ready, or because the thought of doing the work to make real change paralyzes them.

There is a physiological reason change is so hard. Our patterns of belief are habits that begin when we're young, and these habits become so ingrained in us that they create neural pathways in our brains. Think of these neural pathways as hiking trails. The more you think about something, the more worn the path becomes and the easier it feels to travel that path. Neuroscientist Michael Merzenich, referring to Norman Doidge's book, *The Brain That Changes Itself*, says, "practicing a new habit can change hundreds of millions of the connections between the nerve cells in our neural pathways,"[1] which means we can create new neural pathways, and establish new hiking trails, just by thinking new thoughts. Establishing new trails doesn't feel easy at first because you're creating a trail in a field of tall grass. It takes patience and persistence, and it can feel deeply uncomfortable, but it's worth it. You are ready for change. You wouldn't be reading this book if you weren't.

You Need Motivation

Change takes sustained effort, which is why it is so important to be strongly motivated to do the work. According to Dr. Anders Ericsson, a cognitive psychologist who extensively researched performance, motivation is the most significant predictor of success, and that's because when people are motivated, they feel like they have more control over the outcome, they work harder in the face of obstacles, and they are more likely to make lasting change. [2]

Sometimes people start out with one motivation, then when they reflect more deeply, realize they are really motivated by something else. We are all driven to experience positive feelings, but we are even more driven to avoid the negative ones. In other words, pain is a powerful motivator. For example, if you have a goal to improve in an area, let's say to be more productive, but you are also feeling anxiety regularly, you need to address your anxiety before you can move on to improving your productivity.

Catherine's Motivation Story

Catherine came to me for coaching because she wanted to grow her business and make more money. After only a couple of sessions, she realized her deeper motivation was to stop feeling overwhelmed. She wouldn't make much progress toward the goal of growing her business if she didn't first address the issues that were leading her to feel so overwhelmed.

Through the coaching process, Catherine learned that she felt overwhelmed because she had such a strong need for control. She rarely delegated because she didn't think anyone else could do things as well as she did (and she didn't have time to explain), so she ended up doing most of the work herself. She was having a hard time keeping up with all her responsibilities and knew something had to change. Once she gained clarity about the deeper issues keeping her from growing her business (her need to control was causing her pain), she was more intrinsically motivated to make changes quickly. That's because pain is a more powerful motivator than pleasure. This discovery propelled Catherine to focus on the things she needed to do to let go a little. She learned how to trust and empower others and to prioritize. Catherine ended up increasing her business by 25% in one year, not by focusing solely on her business but by focusing on the emotions that were getting in the way of her success.

Let's Get Real

Ask yourself this question: *If I got brutally honest with myself, what would have to change in my life for me to feel truly happy and at peace?*

Often, the reason people don't make progress toward their goals is because they haven't identified and faced the root cause of what's holding them back. The first step toward positive change is to get honest with yourself about what's been keeping you from taking action toward your goals. Reaching this point takes dedication to living your life with honesty, which may feel uncomfortable at first. Once you take that leap and walk through the discomfort, you will begin to build momentum. That momentum will propel you to achieve great things and to feel alive.

EXERCISE: Motivation

What's your motivation for doing this work?

- Do you want to feel more peace and joy in your life?
- Do you want to make more money?
- Do you want to have more balance?
- Do you want to have better relationships?
- Do you want to feel more confident?

Is there anything standing in your way that you need to address first?

I want to:

_____.

_____is causing me pain or stress,
therefore needs to be addressed first.

CHAPTER 3

YOUR EMOTIONAL NEEDS

This book isn't about rehashing the past. It's about being honest with yourself about how your past may be impacting the way you show up in the present, and then letting go of its hold over you.

At the end of chapter two, you identified the feeling that's causing you pain or stress. This feeling is an important clue to help you understand your needs. You have subconscious emotional patterns that started when you were a child to meet your most fundamental needs—to feel connected, safe, and worthy. These three emotional needs drove your actions when you were young—and if you're honest with yourself, these needs still drive many of your actions.

Our Need to Feel Connected (Loved)

Your task is not to seek for love, but merely to seek and find all the barriers within yourself that you have built against it.

—Rumi, 13th century Persian poet

Definition of Connection:

The feeling that we belong to a group and feel close to other people. Someone cares about us and has affection for us.

Human beings are wired to connect with one another. Babies are born dependent on others to survive, and not just for food and shelter. Studies show that babies without a primary, nurturing caregiver have a much higher mortality rate than average infants. This was first proven in the 1940s by Austrian psychoanalyst René Spitz. Spitz compared a group of infants raised in orphanages, with limited human interaction, to a group of infants raised in prison nurseries with regular contact with their mothers and other children. Of the babies raised in the orphanages, 37% died, while there were no deaths in the prison cohort. The babies raised in prison nurseries were physically healthier, grew more quickly, had better motor skills, and scored higher on intelligence tests than the babies who survived in the orphanages. [3]

As we grow, love and connection remain crucial to our development and well-being. Studies in adults show that "lack of human connection can be more harmful to your health than obesity, smoking and high blood pressure."[4] In his book, *Social: Why Our Brains Are Wired to Connect*, Matthew D. Lieberman, neuroscientist, and professor in UCLA's Department of Psychology, writes about the importance of human connection: "Our brains evolved to experience threats to our social connections in much the same way they experience physical pain, by activating the same neural circuitry that causes us to feel pain. The neural link between social and physical pain also ensures that staying socially connected will be a lifelong need."[5]

Over the past few decades, people have become more isolated, especially in Western society. We're less apt to rely on a large extended family, friends, and neighbors for support. We're taught that we can make it on our own and that it's good to be self-sufficient. We're more connected to our

12

phones than to people. We may have hundreds of *friends* on social media but can go days without really connecting with the people who matter most to us. Because of the way our brains are wired, this leaves us feeling like something's missing. In his book, *From Strength to Strength*, Arthur C. Brooks cites an 80-year Harvard study that concluded that happiness comes from loving other human beings.[6] It's that simple.

Even people who have caring friends and families can feel a level of emptiness that leads to anxiety. That's how Isaac was feeling when he came to me for coaching, although he would never have admitted it to himself at the time. He told me his goal was to improve his leadership skills and make more money. Isaac had recently been promoted to the executive team at the software company where he worked. He had a loving wife, three young children, and a very large network of people he kept in touch with regularly. He was well-liked because he had a generous and open personality and really wanted to help others and make a difference. On paper, he had it all.

I quickly came to sense that Isaac wasn't being honest with himself about what he was really feeling. He kept repeating the same phrases, "I'm sick and tired of other people's drama," and, "All I do for you, and this is what I get?" He was increasingly overwhelmed by his work and family responsibilities, and he was annoyed and resentful of people around him. Instead of addressing his concerns, he kept them bottled up, and his resentment began to consume and exhaust him. When we met, he was about to explode. His relationship with his wife wasn't where he wanted it to be, and he was having issues with a couple of his work colleagues.

As with most people, Isaac's biggest strength was also his biggest weakness. He was a pleaser. It made him feel good to help others so he did what he could to be there for them, but if a challenge or disagreement occurred, he avoided it. His inability to honestly communicate his feelings led him to become resentful and overwhelmed. It also frustrated people around him. This pattern wasn't new. Isaac had always had a very close relationship with his father and strived to please him. From a young age, he worked hard to make his father proud by becoming a star athlete and exceptional student. Here is how Isaac explained it: *"I never wanted to let my father down so if the chips were down for me in any aspect of my life, I would either ignore, avoid, or mask in order to save face with my father. This was very unhealthy as it seeped into many aspects of my life as an adult."*

Isaac's old pattern was hurting him. Through the coaching process, he learned that when he didn't allow himself to express his feelings, he wasn't being real with people. By assuming others would react negatively, he didn't give them the opportunity to speak their truth. This put a barrier between him and other people, and as a result, he lost countless opportunities to connect on a deeper level. By avoiding tough conversations, Isaac was getting the opposite result of what he wanted most.

Isaac didn't want to live that way anymore because he valued his relationships more than anything else. He made a commitment to himself that he would work hard to learn how to communicate openly and create boundaries. It felt uncomfortable because he wasn't used to addressing issues head on and because he was so used to putting himself last. He realized it was OK to have needs and to express those needs to people he cared about. The tough work Isaac did liberated him from his old, limiting patterns, and made him feel better about himself and his relationships.

Isaac's story demonstrates how masking your emotions can keep you from having deep connections. It's critical to be honest with yourself and others about your feelings, to be willing to set boundaries, and to say no when your gut is telling you to.

Our Need to Feel Safe/Secure

The root of suffering is resisting the certainty that no matter what the circumstances, uncertainty is all we truly have.

—Pema Chodron, American-Tibetan Buddhist

Definition of Safety:

To feel secure that we won't suffer physical or emotional pain. No matter what happens, we'll be OK.

Early humans were vulnerable to harm from a variety of animals, harsh elements, and other humans. Because of those pervasive threats, they had to remain hyper-vigilant. Like our prehistoric ancestors, we have a strong need to feel safe and secure. Our brains and nervous systems evolved to alert us to anything that could cause us physical pain or threaten our well-being, which led to an intricate system of responses, including fight, flight, or freeze.

Some people can never seem to satisfy their need to feel secure. There's always an underlying fear that they're not going to have enough or that they'll lose what they have. Sometimes these fears can become irrational. Many of my clients have everything they need but still obsess over money.

We all have a strong need to feel safe and secure, but if we suffered trauma or neglect, our need for safety may be more pronounced. If our parents were cold, absent, or inattentive, we didn't get this need met at the level we required. Even if we had parents who loved us and showed it, they may not have met our need for safety as consistently as we needed it. Parents are human, sometimes they feel stressed out and overwhelmed. Sometimes they have money concerns or relationship problems. All this impacted us as children.

When this need is unmet or met in sporadic ways, children will find small ways to make themselves feel secure–by taking control of what they can, by becoming people pleasers, or perfectionists, and by keeping their real feelings to themselves so no one can hurt them.

This need shows up with many of my clients, even the most successful ones. Lina was the Chief Operations Officer at an insurance company when we met. The CEO hired me to coach her because of several complaints he'd received about her. Lina was highly intelligent, and she had years of experience in operations in a variety of industries. She was good at creating processes, and she had a knack for coaching her staff.

She showed up much differently with people outside her department, especially if they questioned her methods or didn't follow her plan. When that happened, she got defensive and would either go on the attack or quietly seethe. She wasn't aware of how her intensity made other people feel. She would often think, "I know what's best here, if they would only do it my way, they would see that."

Just like Isaac, this pattern came from her childhood. Lina's father left at a young age and her mother was an alcoholic. She and her siblings never knew what to expect, including angry outbursts or days of being left alone to fend for themselves. They walked on eggshells all the time.

Being the oldest, she learned to take care of herself and her siblings. She cooked, cleaned, and made sure everyone got to school on time. Since there was so much uncertainty at home, she developed behaviors that made her feel secure; she became a highly organized perfectionist, and she excelled at school. She made an unconscious decision that she had to take care of herself because she couldn't rely on other people. She overdeveloped the part of her personality that took control and got things done as a way to protect herself and to give her the safety and security she didn't get from her mother.

As an adult, Lina was serious and controlling. She didn't know how to let go and have fun, and she never learned the skills to compromise. She gave off an intense energy without realizing it. When we dug deeper into her patterns, we learned that the reason she was more nurturing with her staff was because she felt safe with them, she was in a position of authority and she had nothing to prove, so she could relax. With other people, she had her guard up, always on the lookout for possible threats.

Lina worked hard to release her need for control, not because her boss wanted her to but because it was hurting her. She had been feeling isolated and anxious but didn't know why. The tools that worked when she was young couldn't keep up with the complexities she faced as an adult.

The first step Lina took to change was to become aware that this pattern was a blind spot she developed when she was young to meet her need for security. The young part of her that developed this pattern was trying to protect her and keep her safe the only way it knew how. Instead of feeling ashamed about it, though, she could appreciate what it was trying to do and use it as an opportunity to grow.

Most of the tools we use to feel safe and secure isolate us and keep us from connecting with others. Here are some examples:

- We put walls up and pretend we're fine when we don't feel that way.
- We don't communicate what we really feel.
- We tell ourselves we don't need help from anyone.
- We become perfectionists so we feel like we have control over our environment.
- We judge others.
- We judge ourselves.

The irony is that connection with other human beings is the best way to feel secure, that's what feeds our souls. The starting point of connection is vulnerability. My definition of vulnerability is simple: allowing ourselves to be authentic with others, showing up the way we really are, warts and all. Most of us are uncomfortable getting vulnerable because it leaves us exposed.

From my experience working with my clients, I can tell you that vulnerability begets vulnerability. When you are vulnerable, it alerts the other person's subconscious that you're safe. True leadership is the willingness to go first. To face your fears and to act anyway. You'll be surprised at what you get back.

The most effective way to get vulnerable, even when it feels uncomfortable, is to practice compassion for ourselves and others. It's easier to feel compassion when we remember that each of us is doing our best to fulfill the same needs, to feel loved, safe, and worthy.

Our Need to Feel Worthy

No one can make you feel inferior without your consent.

—Eleanor Roosevelt

Definition of Worthy:

The feeling that we're good enough just the way we are, no matter what we do, how we look, or what we have. We deserve love simply for existing.

We all need to feel worthy, like we matter to someone and that our time on this earth means something. It's easier to see this need in other people than it is to see it in ourselves. No one wants to admit that they need to feel significant or that they overcompensate because on some level, they don't feel good enough. This need comes up a lot in the work I do with my clients. Sometimes it presents itself loud and clear, other times more subtly. There are so many ways people learned to feel good enough:

- By being the best at school or sports
- By making their parents proud
- By working the hardest
- By making the most money
- By being the nicest
- By controlling situations
- By being the best parent
- By judging others
- By judging themselves
- By becoming perfectionists

- By becoming people pleasers

- By being the best at details

- By pretending they can handle anything

- By not being honest about their needs

- By trying to control what people think of them

At first, I thought maybe this need was showing up more with my clients because they were high achievers, with parents that expected a lot from them. Then I remembered that my clients came from all types of backgrounds. So, I began observing everyone I knew, starting with myself, and I saw this need cropping up again and again. I noticed kids in just about every family competing with their siblings for attention and approval, even in families where their parents gave them lots of positive attention. I saw how much time and energy my daughter and her friends invested in posting just the right photo to Instagram, and how the comments all centered around looks. I saw so many adults spending countless hours making themselves crazy on social media by comparing their lives to the carefully curated stories other people posted. I noticed how much validation I sought from others, especially my clients, and how angry I got at myself when I made a mistake.

So many people have a part of themselves that doesn't feel good enough. We're constantly comparing ourselves to others. That's not how we started out though. We started out unencumbered and complete.

Marianne Williamson puts it beautifully in her book, *A Return to Love*: "As children we were taught to be good boys and girls, which of course implies we were not that already. We were taught we're good if we clean up our room or we're good if we make good grades, but very few of us were taught that we're essentially good. Very few of us were given a sense of unconditional approval, a feeling that we were precious because of what we are, not what we do, and that's not because we were raised by monsters, we were raised by people who were raised the same way we were."[7]

If our parents were hard on us, they had parents who were hard on them. If they were critical or aloof, they had parents who were the same way. Human beings have children, and human beings are flawed. If they tried to be perfect parents, they failed because there's no such thing.

You may be thinking this need doesn't apply to you because you feel confident. The truth is you can feel confident but still crave approval. It doesn't mean you're walking around feeling bad about yourself all the time, this need is usually far below the surface. It drives us even when we're not aware it's driving us. Even legends have this need. In "The Last Dance," an incredible documentary about basketball superstar Michael Jordan, he talks about how strongly his need for his father's approval drove him. He said, "I always felt like I was fighting Larry (his brother) for my father's attention. When you're going through it, it's traumatic because I wanted that approval. So, my determination got even greater to be as good if not better than my brother."[8]

We finally feel worthy when we no longer need to prove ourselves to anyone. When we're confident that we're enough, no matter what we do or what we have. I know this is easier said than done because I'm a recovering validation-seeker, myself. I learned that this need was coming from a deep place within me that was telling me I wasn't good enough, and that made me judge people as a way to feel better about myself. I came to realize only recently that I judged myself the hardest. I was craving approval from others to prove to *myself* that I was good enough. Learning to love myself helped stop this constant need for validation. It took time and patience to practice self-compassion, and it's a work in progress, but repeating these statements has made a big difference.

- You are worthy of love just the way you are.

- You deserve good things in your life without having to suffer for them.

- You don't need to change who you are to make people like you or to achieve success.

- You are not weak if you admit you're wrong—there is power in humility, and there is humanity in failure.

- Your mistakes are gifts on your path to success.

All three emotional needs— to feel loved, secure, and worthy—are a natural part of life. They are present in all humans, so there's nothing wrong with having them. It's the way we meet them that matters. We can meet these needs in more productive ways, ways that make us feel good about ourselves and help society. The healthiest ways to fulfill these needs are to practice compassion and to become present in each moment. I will get into more detail about how to do this later.

Our Three Emotional Needs Can Lead to Blind Spots

Blind spots are aspects of our personality that are obvious to everyone but us. They're things we do that limit us, or make other people feel bad. They're subconscious actions or habits such as interrupting, reacting impulsively, avoiding, playing the victim, getting defensive, hiding, blaming, making assumptions, micromanaging, judging, posturing, masking, reacting vs. listening, and so on. Even people who are self-aware have blind spots.

Our blind spots are often formed when we're young to help us meet our emotional needs. For instance, someone who felt ignored as a kid may become a know-it-all when they're older. Someone who felt it was impossible to live up to their father's expectations may be hard on themselves as an adult.

One of my blind spots was managing people. Sometimes I did that by interrupting and redirecting, other times I did it by having an answer for everything. I'll never forget the moment I was made aware of it. I was attending a coach training retreat where we learned how to coach others by uncovering our own baggage. Each of us underwent intense analysis of our emotional patterns, focusing on how our past traumas showed up in our lives as adults.

I was at a dinner with the group on our second day. My coach and the facilitator of the program were sitting across from me, talking. I interrupted them because I thought the facilitator had said something about me. I don't remember what I thought she was talking about, but I must have corrected her because she said, "Amal, that's not what I was talking about. I'm going to be honest with you because that's why you're here. I've noticed that you constantly try to run interference with people and manage their perceptions of you. You have an almost desperate need for people to like you and to have control." This feedback wasn't easy to hear, and I felt like I was about to cry, like I got in trouble. I held it together and remained quiet for the rest of the evening.

When I reflected on what she said, I knew she was right. I eavesdropped on conversations to make sure people weren't talking about me— as if I could even control that. I had been oblivious to how much this blind spot impacted people's perception of me: I was coming off as insecure and desperate, the exact opposite result of the one I wanted.

This blind spot came from my belief that I wasn't good enough. That feeling disconnected me from people, because I always had my guard up and I put image above connection. I didn't trust people because I didn't really trust myself.

I see some form of this with many of my clients. They don't feel good enough and that manifests in different ways, often leading to distinct blind spots. Do any of the following examples resonate with you?

- Charlotte was a perfectionist and she liked to be in charge. She felt anxiety about all the things she needed to do, a feeling she tried to manage by planning and making lists down to the smallest detail. Then she would ruminate for days about things that wouldn't go as planned. She had two blind spots that were related to her need to have things just so: she would get bossy with people about the plan, and she would take small things personally if anyone questioned her plan.

- James didn't feel comfortable being himself around people. He believed for years that if he was really himself, people wouldn't like him. From the time he was in middle school, he thought he had to be outgoing and "work" the crowd. He learned to talk and tell stories. This led to his blind spot of talking over people and rambling on and on. The overwhelming feedback he received from his peers was that he didn't take social cues when people were done listening. He was talking at people rather than having meaningful exchanges.

- Paul was the youngest of four boys. His brothers teased him relentlessly when they were growing up. As an adult he was the most successful of all his brothers. He had everything he'd ever wanted, a thriving law practice, two homes, a boat, and a loving family. He was an amazing father and husband, and his partners and staff had a high level of respect for him. But people were often bothered by how much Paul bragged, especially when he got together with his brothers. In their company, he reverted to the same patterns from his youth, bragging and competing to the point that his brothers finally called him out on it. They told him his bragging was pushing them away.

The best leaders continuously investigate their blind spots and solicit feedback to develop and grow. Here are some of the most common blind spots I've seen with leaders:

- They say they're open to feedback but don't want to hear bad news.

- They delegate, then micromanage.

- They create silos by communicating to each individual in private vs. creating an open, transparent culture.

- They don't address bad behavior among their employees or colleagues, which can contribute to a toxic environment.

- They can't admit when they're wrong.

- They say they're transparent, but don't have tough conversations when necessary.

> The nature of blind spots is that we are unaware of them. Great leaders make it their mission to investigate and uncover their blind spots.

Everyone has blind spots. Some people avoid, others get resentful, angry, annoyed, or controlling. What do you think your #1 blind spot is? If you don't know, it's time to start getting curious because our blind spots can cause conflict. Most of all, they make us feel bad about ourselves and limit our growth.

EXERCISE: Ask Your Friends to Identify Your Blind Spots

There is no need to get embarrassed or feel bad—we all have blind spots. Once you do the work to become conscious of them, you can address them and minimize their negative consequences.

Think of three to five people who know you well, and who will be *honest* with you. Ask them the following questions:

1. *How do I act when I am under stress, pressure, or a deadline?*
2. *How does this behavior affect you or others?*

Write down what you hear and try to identify a pattern.

What is your blind spot?

Which of the three needs is driving your blind spot (safety, connection, worthiness)? It may be more than one.

Is there a more empowering way to meet this need?

CHAPTER 4

YOUR SUBCONSCIOUS MAP

The best way to release the past's hold over you is to become conscious of your Map.

Your Map is the pattern of emotions, beliefs, and behaviors you subconsciously created in childhood to meet your need to feel worthy, loved, and secure.

Our Map helps define our perspective about life, and that's where problems can emerge because we're often unable to see that others have their own perspectives. We think our perspective is reality, but it's just *our* reality. When we have a hard time getting along with someone or understanding where they're coming from, it's often because we're filtering their perspective through our own Map, rather than seeing their unique view of the situation.

Human beings aren't perfect, and neither are their Maps. One of the reasons our Maps are flawed is because they were scrawled out long before our brains were fully developed. Think of ourselves at twelve, or nine, or even four years old. We made decisions with the tools we had at hand. In our attempt to avoid pain and keep ourselves from feeling insignificant, our young minds often misjudge reality because the part of the brain that controls our survival instinct and regulates emotions—the amygdala—is highly active in childhood. The prefrontal cortex, the rational part of the brain that makes logical decisions, isn't fully developed until around age 25.

What does that mean? Sometimes our young minds made big, sweeping conclusions about people and events that seemed true, but were part of a flawed Map. For example, let's say when you were nine years old, your best friend lied to you. She swore she wouldn't tell a secret that you shared with her, but then she did. She told just about everyone in your school. What happens? Your amygdala jumps into action and tells you, "People can't be trusted." And you believe it.

What's in a Map?

Our Maps are made up of three elements: our beliefs, our mantras, and our rules. We have a variety of thoughts and beliefs, some positive and some negative. We're focusing on the negative ones here, the ones that limit us or cause us pain so we can learn how to shift our mindsets and feel happier.

- **Limiting Beliefs**: Anything we believe that hurts us, hurts someone else, or limits our positive influence on others. We stand by our beliefs even if they're not true.

    ◊ **Example**: "I don't fit in anywhere because I'm not good enough."

- **Negative Mantras**: The things we say to ourselves over and over. Limiting beliefs generate negative mantras.

    ◊ **Example**: "They're talking about me."

- **Rules:** How we judge the world and the people in it. What we think needs to happen in our life. How we think people need to act, treat us, and treat other people. Limiting beliefs, over time, turn into limiting rules.

    ◊ **Example**: "If someone respects me, they won't disagree with me."

Limiting Beliefs & Mantras

A belief is a conviction that something is true. Limiting beliefs are any beliefs you have that do just that, limit you, cause you stress or anxiety or inhibit your growth and positive influence with other people. Most of us don't question our beliefs, but instead focus lots of energy on reinforcing them by repeating them in our head in the form of mantras. Mantras can be empowering, positive messages, or negative messages, including worries, doubts, and judgments. We repeat these mantras subconsciously, and the negative ones are often harsher than anything we would say out loud or to a friend. Negative mantras (*I'm so stupid*, or *What the hell is wrong with these people?*) lead to negative feelings toward ourselves and others. This can happen even if we think we're being careful about what we say, because studies show that up to 93% of our communication is nonverbal.[9]

What we focus on grows. If we repeat negative mantras in our heads, we get negative results. When we focus on things that make us feel worried and stressed, what happens? Our bodies produce cortisol, and we feel more worried and more stressed. When we focus on what other people aren't doing right, or what they're doing to us, or how they're letting us down, those things magnify. Anything can become a self-fulfilling prophecy.

When I meet with a new client, I write down the phrases they repeat. After a couple of weeks, I share my list with them, and they're often surprised at how frequently they repeat certain phrases. We're usually able to uncover a theme together by relating what they repeatedly say to the emotions they're feeling.

Remember, your limiting beliefs generate negative mantras, so if you become aware of what you repeat to yourself, you can get a better understanding of the deeper beliefs driving those statements. It's not always easy to identify your limiting beliefs because they are deep-rooted in your subconscious. It may be helpful to enlist a friend, mentor, or coach to help you.

Tony's Mantras

My client Tony is a successful entrepreneur who came to me feeling unfocused and burned out. He was another client who looked like he had it all—financial success, physical health, and a loving family, but that was only half the story. Tony had spent much of his 25 years as a business owner feeling frustrated and depleted. He rarely felt productive, no matter how many hours he worked. Tony had a few mantras he would repeat in his head during the course of the day:

"These people are clueless!"

"Here we go again."

"I have to do everything around here!"

> What you say in your head is typically much harsher
> than what you say out loud.

Tony wasn't aware he had these phrases stuck on repeat, yet they were impacting his level of influence with others. For example, when an employee named Alex, whom Tony frequently got frustrated with, would make a mistake, Tony would think, *What the hell is wrong with you? I have to do everything myself if I want it done right.* Although he would never say those things out loud, he would act annoyed, then take care of the mistake himself. Not surprisingly, Tony's behavior did little to improve morale or productivity at his company ... and it didn't make him feel good about himself as a leader. He wasn't enjoying his work because he was on edge so often, and since people were uncomfortable approaching him for fear of his reaction, he felt isolated.

Laura's Mantras

Laura, a vice president at a healthcare company, was smart and capable, but she lacked confidence. Similar to Isaac in chapter three, she never wanted to let anyone down, so she took on too much responsibility. She was a people-pleaser who wanted to show others she had it all together, she rarely said no to anything, and she didn't communicate when something was bothering her. She often repeated the following mantras:

"I am really busy!"

"I'm the only one who can get this done."

"I don't have any balance in my life!"

"Did I do it right?"

Laura was uncomfortable with conflict, and as a result, avoided difficult conversations. She developed profound feelings of frustration, anxiety, and resentment, which hurt her relationships. Laura often ended up in the weeds, both at home and at work. Although she projected an image of reliability, lots of things fell through the cracks because she refused to delegate or say no. As a result, people in her life concluded that she was unreliable. As in so many of the previous examples, she was getting the opposite result of the one she wanted most.

> What we say in our head impacts how we feel
> and how we make other people feel.

Tony's and Laura's mantras were limiting them. These mantras were part of a larger problem—a Map that no longer supported them. Their Maps, like mine, were rooted in old patterns, which needed to change if they wanted to improve their lives.

My Mantras

Some of the negative mantras I said to myself were:

"They're judging me."

"What's wrong with them?"

"What's wrong with me?"

"I need to snap out of it."

"I can't take it anymore."

Before I did the work to uncover the parts of my Map that were limiting me, some variation of this messaging was running through my mind constantly. Like Tony and Laura, I used mantras as subconscious coping mechanisms. I wasn't aware I was repeating them, but they were always there, below the surface, affecting my response to virtually every situation I faced.

EXERCISE: Identify Your Mantras & Limiting Beliefs

Commit to paying close attention to the things you repeat to yourself or out loud. Keep a notebook handy or use your phone to jot down the statements that keep cropping up.

Ask someone you spend a lot of time with to help you. You can make a game out of it. At first, you may be identifying mantras, but that's good, your mantras will give you clues about your limiting beliefs. Have patience with yourself, identifying your inner dialogue can take time. Sometimes the things we say to ourselves are so deeply rooted in our subconscious that we don't even realize we're repeating them.

Rules

Rules are judgments we make about the world, about how people should act and how they should treat us. We learn some of our rules from our parents or caregivers, and others from our own experiences. Some rules are positive and motivating, like the ubiquitous "golden rule": treat others the way you want to be treated. There are other rules, though, that can have a negative impact on our lives and relationships, even rules that seem benign. For example, Julie, a Human Resource Leader at a large university, uncovered one of her rules when she realized that she'd failed to catch an error on an important contract she had signed off on. She called me freaking out and blaming her colleague, who helped draft the contract. Her energy seemed frantic. I asked her why she was so upset. She told me she prided herself on doing the right thing and having integrity. I reminded her that this was a mistake, that she and her colleague were human and it's a good thing they found the error so they could fix the mistake.

She agreed but couldn't let go of her anger and blame. Here's how our conversation went:

Me: What's the worst thing that could happen?

Julie: I could get in trouble.

Me: Then what?

Julie: I could get fired.

Me: Then what?

Julie: I won't have enough money.

Me: Then what?

Julie: That would be the worst thing in life, I would rather get run over by a truck.

Me: I bet you have enough money in savings, don't you?

Julie: I have more money in savings than most of the people I know.

Julie had a high need for security, to the point where no level of financial stability was enough to make her feel truly secure. This pattern makes sense when you look at her Map. She had suffered emotional trauma and neglect when she was young. This had led to an underlying feeling that she needed to protect herself, and one of the ways she learned to do that was by working hard and making money.

Her rule was, "If I make a mistake, then I could get in trouble."

This rule led her to make small issues bigger than they needed to be. It created lots of anxiety and fear for her and made other people think she overreacted. This pattern isn't unique to Julie. Although we wouldn't want to admit we have a fear of "getting in trouble," it's common. We tie our basic emotional need for security to how much money we have.

After years of working to understand my own Map, I experienced a breakthrough that helped me heal an old wound I didn't even know I had. My daughter was weeks away from leaving for her first year of college. I had been feeling really down that summer but couldn't understand why. I figured it had something to do with her leaving because I was having all these memories come up from her childhood, particularly all the regrets I had as a mother. I thought, I should have spent more time with her, I shouldn't have been so hard on her, and I should have been more laid back and easygoing. I didn't even think about all the good things I had done that led to our close and loving relationship. At the same time, I began having weird thoughts about my mortality. I fixated on all the lonely elderly people I saw and would say to myself, "I'm going to end up like that." Instead of witnessing these feelings and acknowledging them as a natural response to a major life change, I fought hard against them. I kept saying, "I need to snap out of it," and "what the hell is wrong with me?"

It came to a head when we were on vacation. My daughter was on edge all weekend and had snapped at me a few times. I was also feeling edgy and after a small disagreement, I called her bitch. Even before the word left my mouth, I wanted to take it back. Our relationship was based on mutual respect, and we never spoke to each other that way. I called my friend sobbing, "What the hell's wrong with me? I've got to snap of it!" She said, "Why are you being so hard on yourself? I said, "Hard on myself? What kind of mother acts like this?" Instantly she said, "Stop trying to control everything. You're not allowing yourself to be human. Showing your emotions, doesn't mean you're weak." That's when it hit me, I was breaking a rule I didn't even know I had: In order to be loved, I had to be perfect, and if I showed weakness (emotions) that meant I wasn't perfect.

If someone I cared about had that rule, I would feel compassion for them. Why couldn't I have that same compassion for myself? This question started me on the path to healing. Later that day, I apologized to my daughter and told her how much I was struggling with letting go. We both cried, and then we had the first of several amazing conversations.

EXERCISE: What Are Your Rules?

It's time for you to become conscious of how your mantras and beliefs could be leading to limiting rules. Rules are usually "if/then" statements. If [this thing happens] then [that thing will happen]. My example: If I'm perfect, then I'll be loved.

1. Think of a situation that happened recently in which you felt angry, sad, or frustrated. Were you operating from a rule?

2. How is this rule hurting you?

It can be tricky to identify your rules and how they limit you, so don't be too hard on yourself if you come up with nothing at first. It's a process, and it takes time. If you work with a therapist or coach, they may be able to help you.

CHAPTER 5

OUR PAST IMPACTS OUR PRESENT

Here's Where My Map Came From

It was a beautiful fall day. The air was crisp, the sun was shining, and my friend Kelly and I were raking leaves in my front yard and talking about eighth grade topics like cheerleading and football games. Suddenly we heard a loud noise coming from up the street, which was unusual for my normally quiet neighborhood. Five black cars came speeding down my street, screeching to a halt in front of my house. The car doors burst open, and men in blue suits and serious expressions started running furiously toward our front door, past me and Kelly. The man in charge stopped in front of me and ordered, "Your friend needs to go home now."

The next thing I remember was sitting at my dining room table with my parents. The men in suits, I learned, were federal agents, and they were searching our house. My father had gone pale. I looked over at my mother and saw that her expression was very different, solemn, and dignified. I started crying. It was a little forced because that's what I thought I was supposed to do. "Stop crying, Amal," my father pleaded. He looked scared, and I could tell he didn't want to upset the agents, so I stopped.

We sat there in silence. I was confused, but I don't remember feeling particularly worried. I thought, *"This is all some sort of mistake. They can search the house, but they won't find whatever it is they are looking for, and they'll leave, and everything will be fine. We didn't do anything wrong."*

After a couple of hours, it finally looked like the agents were about ready to leave, and my parents seemed to relax slightly, but I knew they were anxious to show the men the door. The agent in command approached my mother and said her name, loud and slow.

"Yes," she answered, her tone surprised but stoic.

"You are under arrest. We won't cuff you because of the neighbors."

I heard her say, "Cuff me, I don't care."

But her face told me she did care. I tried to make eye contact with her, but she wouldn't meet my gaze. I watched her being taken away in the back of one of those black cars.

My mom was one of several people arrested that day in a federal sting operation tracking an international drug trafficking ring. The story was featured that night on national news in living rooms across America. After spending six months in a federal prison in New York City during the trial, my mother was acquitted. Although she had been associating with people who were found guilty, there was no evidence to prove that she did anything illegal. In my mind though, she was guilty of taking something precious from me, something I would never get back: my innocence, my youth, and my carefree spirit.

When I returned to school in the agonizing days following my mother's arrest, I felt a deep shame that never really went away. Who could blame me? I was in the stage of life when nothing matters more than what people think of you, and the whole school was talking about me and my family. I went from being an optimistic, confident, free-spirited kid with friends from different social groups to being a suspicious, insecure kid with a fast-dwindling number of friends. I went from being happy and curious to being anxious, and distrustful of anyone I thought was judging me. I wouldn't have dared to show that I was feeling that way inside though, and I became impressively skilled at acting, at pretending everything was fine and that I was happy. I never once shared how I was feeling with anyone, nor did I even consider it an option.

Secrets Hurt Us

It's not easy for me to talk about this story because I kept it a secret for most of my life. I was worried that people would judge me or that they wouldn't see me in the same way. Also, I was protective of my mother. This story portrays her negatively, and she was so much more than that. She was full of love and life, and she raised five kids with not much support from my dad. She did the best she could with the Map she was given.

The first time I spoke about this story out loud was with my own coach when I was 40 years old. I cried so much I could barely get the words out. It was visceral—my body had conspired with my mind for so long to keep this secret that when I was finally letting it go, it felt deeply uncomfortable and disorienting. I could barely breathe, and my heart was racing.

I eventually learned that this secret was related to my need to keep every aspect of my life under control. I had worked really hard to manage people's perceptions of me, and I didn't know how much energy that took until I began to loosen up a little. It's not like I was consciously keeping this secret, though. I didn't walk around telling myself that I couldn't let people know the truth about my past. Most of the time, I didn't even think about it. It wasn't until I let go of the secret that I learned how much it had been haunting me.

Just because we're successful at pushing things out of our conscious minds doesn't mean they aren't lurking in the background impacting our relationships. We're wired to connect with other people. When we hold on to secrets, our ability to connect diminishes because people can sense, at some level, that we're not being authentic. But it's the challenges and pain of life that can make us interesting, and that can attract people to us.

I'm not suggesting that you should spill your guts about the intimate details of your life. That's not realistic or appropriate in most instances. I am telling you to spend time and energy paying attention to how you portray yourself. Most people cultivate a sort of character that's safe for others to see, fearing that people won't like them if they are really themselves. This is exhausting. There is tremendous power in letting go of caring what people think about us.

Our Past Impacts the Way We Show Up as Adults

There were other early experiences in my life that contributed to my emotional patterns. I was the youngest of five children, and there was a big age difference between me and the rest of my siblings. I often felt like an afterthought, like I wasn't heard, and like my ideas and thoughts didn't matter. By the time I was born, my parents were too tired to give me the attention and approval I craved.

The raid on our home stands out for me, in part, because it was so dramatic, of course, but also because it happened at a time when I was experiencing the difficulties of adolescence. There's rarely just one event that shapes us though. Often, it's thousands of little things. But this book isn't about rehashing the past, it's about being honest with yourself about how your past may be impacting the way you show up in the present and then letting go of its hold on you.

If there's something from your past that you've been pushing out of your mind or resisting, it may be time for you to do some work to face it. This kind of work will help you release deep patterns that cause you pain and limit your ability to live life as fully as you deserve. Don't try to do it alone, though, because past traumas can be triggering. It's best to find a licensed therapist to help you face these in a safe environment, at a pace that's comfortable for you. If you aren't willing or able to talk to a therapist, you may want to read Gabrielle Bernstein's book, *Happy Days: The Guided Path from Trauma to Profound Inner Peace*. It's filled with tools and techniques for dealing with past trauma safely.

Is It Your Map or Someone Else's?

For years, I was hard on people. I judged them in my head, and I lashed out when things didn't go my way. My biggest trigger was feeling unheard or disrespected. The smallest thing could set me off. This pattern limited me in so many ways, but most of all it made me anxious. When I became conscious of the pattern, I could see that I was acting just like my mother had acted when I was young. I was acting in a way that I hated, a way that had made me feel like I was walking on eggshells as a kid. As an adult, I saw my children and husband reacting to me in the same way. That was a hard realization, and it was one of the most powerful motivators for me to change. I knew I had to break the cycle. Changing this pattern was the most difficult thing I've ever done.

Observe anyone you know long enough, and you will get clues about their Map.

Here's a story about my mother that gave me some insight into her Map. One night when I was 11, my parents were having a dinner party. There were more than a dozen people over, most of them sitting in the living room after enjoying the delicious Lebanese feast my mom had made. Everyone was having a good time, laughing, and telling jokes. My mom was busy serving her guests drinks and dessert. Every time she walked by my dad, he pinched her. He thought he was being funny, but she was getting annoyed. After the third time, my mother said, "If you do it again, you'll be sorry." He just laughed. My mom was 5 feet tall and had a skirt and high heels on and my dad was 5'10". Shortly after, she walked by my dad, and he did it again. She grabbed him by the wrist and flipped him over her shoulder. He landed on his back with a loud thud. He was out cold. The guests stared at my mom, flabbergasted. She bent down, yelling his name over and over. She was freaking out because she thought she'd killed him. When he opened his eyes after a couple of minutes, he was barely able to get up. My mom told my brother to take him to the hospital just to make sure he was OK and continued with the dinner party. Years later, she loved telling that story. "I told him not to mess with me," she would say. "You need to be strong because people will try to take advantage of you if you let them."

My mother prided herself on not letting anyone get the best of her. If she liked you, she would do anything to help you, but if you made her feel disrespected in any way, you had better run for cover. She demanded respect. It seems clear now that she met her needs for security and significance by showing that she didn't take shit from anyone. She cultivated a tough persona, out of necessity, which unfortunately meant she spent less energy on learning to communicate.

Rewriting Your Map

Isn't it funny how we can hate something about our parents, then grow up to do the same thing? That's because we learn what we live, even if we don't want to. The reason you're not destined to be the same as your parents, however, is because you have free will.

You can and must re-write your Map. Becoming conscious of your blind spots is the most important first step, but it's not enough to snap out of it in the moment, when you feel triggered.

We're all surprised at some point to learn that we're never done evolving. It's like peeling an onion, one layer at a time. Rewriting your Map requires a commitment to self-discovery, and self-discovery takes an open mind. The first step to re-writing your Map is to identify how you've been meeting your needs to feel connected, safe, and worthy. In the next chapter, we'll use humor to take the shame out of our blind spots, limiting beliefs, and rules.

CHAPTER 6

GETTING TO KNOW YOUR DRAMA MODE™

"The worst of all deceptions is self-deception."

—*Plato*

What's a Drama Mode™?

Your Drama Mode is an emotionally charged persona you create to combat stress, anxiety, shame, anger, or fear. Drama is internal chatter that doesn't accomplish anything but can make you feel better in the short-term. We go into this mode when the chatter takes over, and old limiting patterns of behavior and beliefs get the best of us.

Our Drama Mode comes from what Carl Jung, the founder of analytical psychology, identified as our Shadow, which he explained as inferiorities everybody has but refuses to acknowledge. It's the dark side of our personality, which represents unknown or little-known attributes of the ego.[10] Our Shadow becomes hostile when it's ignored or misunderstood.[11]

Every single one of us has a Shadow. It clouds our judgment, and it makes us present ourselves differently than who we really are. It blocks our potential by telling us to give up on our dreams and goals because they are impossible. Our Shadow comes from fear, and the only way to overcome it is to shine a light on the reasons for that fear.

You are not your Drama Mode! Your Drama Mode is your ego's response to pain, and it's a pattern of emotional tools that have, at times, gotten you the results you've wanted, even if those results were short-term and lower quality than if you weren't in that state of mind.

> We use the word "drama" so we don't fall into the trap
> of taking ourselves too seriously, which makes it easier for us to
> notice and change what's not working.

Don't forget, your Shadow wants you to remain afraid, and your Drama Mode is a tool it uses to keep you there. Becoming aware of your Drama Mode gives you the courage to be your true self. It gives power to the part of you that believes you are capable of anything you put your mind to.

HERE ARE SOME DRAMA MODE EXAMPLES.
DO ANY RESONATE WITH YOU?

Drama Mode	Mantras
Insecure Al/Alice	I work really hard. – Why isn't it recognized? – Am I not good enough?
Walter/Wanda the Wuss	Am I in trouble? – I'm sorry. – Please don't be mad at me.
Paranoid Penny/Pete	Everyone is judging me. – They're out to get me. – Tell me I got it right.
The Whiny Martyr	I'm overwhelmed! – It's not realistic. – I can't rely on anyone else!
Gabe/Gabby The Godfather	You need to respect me! – I'm in charge. – Don't talk to me like that!
Daryl The Defender	You let me down. – That's not fair! – You are wrong, and I can prove it.
Diane/David The Deflector	I am so sick of people's drama. – You're exhausting me. – Deal with your stuff so I don't have to!
The Jerky Judger	These people are idiots! – How do they make it through the day? – I can't work with these people.
Sam/Sally Stepford Wife	I do more in one day than most people do in a week. – Look how hard I work. – I'll work late.
Edgy Elsa/Enzo	Conceal, don't feel. – Why can't you just do it my way? – I'll do it myself.
Eli/Evie Eeyore	Why can't I get any breaks? – I have the worst luck. – Nothing ever goes right for me.

HERE ARE SOME DRAMA MODE EXAMPLES.
DO ANY RESONATE WITH YOU?

Drama Mode	Mantras
Frazzled Frankie	I can't take this anymore! – I'm about to have a breakdown. – I can't handle this.
Debbie/Donny Downer	You don't give me any support. – I can't get the resources I need. – Here's why that won't work.
Suspicious Sammy	People suck. – They can't be trusted. – Everyone is out for themselves.
Passive Pauly/Polly	I work too much. – I don't have time for a personal life. – My life is passing me by.
Know it All Nancy/Ned	Everyone knows that! – Did you think I was stupid? – Well, of COURSE.
Pit Bull Patty/Pauley	What's taking you so long? – Get out of the way. – I'll show you how to do it!
Ron/Ronda the Rescuer (Never Says No)	I can fix it. – You shouldn't have to do that. – Sure, I have time!
The One Upper	I already knew that! – You think that's bad, listen to this one. – I can top that.
The Fixer	I don't like the word DRAMA. – I'm above this. – I'm logical and pragmatic and I help other people deal with their stress.

Naming Your Drama Mode

Naming your Drama Mode helps you remember you are not the drama; that's the first step to neutralizing its power over you. Whereas previously you may have been tempted to say something along the lines of "That's just who I am," or "I can't help it, that's how I feel," once you give the pattern a name, you know that it's the Drama Mode talking!

The list above is just a starting point. It's common to see yourself in more than one of these Drama Modes or to identify with certain aspects of several. What's most important is to become aware of your emotions when a person or event triggers negative self-talk.

Remember, EVERYONE has a Drama Mode™. It's what you do when it appears that matters. Identifying it helps you distance yourself from the old limiting patterns and shift your mindset to feel happier and more confident.

Let's See Some Drama Modes

Tony

During our discussions, it became clear to my client Tony that every time he silently repeated his mantra, *What the hell is wrong with these people?* He was actually in his Drama Mode. Eventually, he chose to call his Drama Mode "Uncle Pauley," a name inspired by a cantankerous family member Tony felt sorry for. He displayed many of the same unattractive traits when he was in his Drama Mode.

"Uncle Pauley is always complaining," he told me, "always judging other people, always finding fault. No one wants to be around him—and that's who I'm being when I act that way. I really don't want to be like that."

Uncle Pauley was not the leader Tony wanted to be, or that Tony's team wanted to deal with. At one point, Tony's employees told me they would cringe at the thought of calling him when there was a problem because of the way he reacted. Tony was not being an effective leader when he showed up in his Drama Mode. He had no idea how his employees felt about him though, because people were afraid to do anything but agree with him.

Because of his personal commitment to improve, Tony worked hard to discover his biggest challenge as a leader. He realized he wasn't communicating well. Instead of identifying clear goals and holding people accountable for fulfilling them, he set vague objectives, then complained when people didn't achieve what he had in mind. Team members inevitably needed help decoding his orders, but when Uncle Pauley was on duty, they weren't going to get it.

Laura

It took Laura longer to identify her Drama Mode, but once she became aware of how strong her need to please was, and how important it was for her to portray perfection, the puzzle pieces began to fall into place. She named her Drama Mode "Sharbie," (a cross between a perfect plastic Barbie doll and an old family friend, Sharon).

Sharon was often angry and resentful and constantly complained about all the work she had to do. Laura had always thought Sharon had a classic martyr complex. So, Laura's Drama Mode was a cross between an unrealistically perfect doll and an angry, resentful complainer.

Here is what Laura noticed: She would start out by attempting to portray perfection, projecting the myth that she could handle anything without complaint or help from anyone. But she eventually discovered that perfection is unrealistic and striving for it made her feel burned-out and easily annoyed. It felt like she was juggling a tray of heavy plates, constantly adding more without putting any down. She focused all her energy on keeping those plates in the air, no matter how heavy they got. Her rules told her that if she dropped one, it meant she wasn't good enough. Sure enough, there came a day when all the plates came crashing down on Laura, and she had to realize that some things in her life needed to change.

In our coaching sessions, Laura discovered how her discomfort expressing her feelings to others was negatively impacting her. In her attempt to be everything to everybody, she showed up as resentful and frustrated. These emotions came from continually putting herself last and creating unrealistic rules about how she wanted to appear to others. When she noticed these rules surfacing, she learned to connect them to Sharbie, the person she became while in her Drama Mode.

Amal

I call my own Drama Mode Lash-Out-Lunatic because she lashes out at inappropriate times. She is focused more on herself than other people, and her anxiety is reflected through anger. Some of my favorite responses to stress included:

- I can't take this anymore!

- I'm overwhelmed!

- It's not realistic!

- I can't rely on anyone else!

They were the hallmarks of the drama I had become addicted to generating. I had to learn to recognize when I was moving into Lash-Out Lunatic territory–which was more often than I realized. Lash-Out Lunatic can still rear her ugly head, but now I know how to kick her to the curb quickly.

It's important to recognize that Drama Modes don't just materialize out of nowhere. Mine helped me manage anxiety and feel significant by finding something I could complain about, or by highlighting how difficult things were for me. It gave me a sense of control whenever I was feeling small or threatened. I would feel the anxiety as an uncomfortable sensation in my chest, and all I knew was that sensation needed to go away. So, I lashed out, and I would feel better for a moment, but I did lasting damage to my relationships.

The further along you go on your path to self-discovery, the more you learn about your patterns. My Lash-Out-Lunatic was my response to the deeper Drama Mode that I was hesitant to address. The one I touched on earlier when I told you how hard I was on myself. Like Laura, I didn't feel good enough, and because of that feeling, I created the rule that I needed to be perfect to be loved. I've only recently become aware of this pattern, and I've named the Drama Mode Sergeant Pain because it's like a drill sergeant–pushing me to perfection, instead of allowing me to give myself grace. This Drama Mode has kept me from learning how to be kind to myself. It has given me a false sense of control and hasn't allowed me to honestly feel my emotions. I'll get into more detail about what this pattern has taught me later in the book.

What Are You Getting Out of Your Drama Mode?

Your Drama Mode wouldn't exist if you weren't getting some benefit from it. Perhaps it:

- Gives you a feeling of control in situations where you feel powerless.
- Let's you escape accountability or blame.
- Keeps the focus on you.
- Helps you to feel significant, like you matter.
- Gives you an excuse for not failing/trying.
- Allows you not to feel uncomfortable emotions.
- Helps you to feel safe.
- Keeps you from having to look too closely at things that aren't working in your life.

EXERCISE: Identify Your Drama Mode

The best way to identify your Drama Mode is to begin by clarifying what three emotions you feel when you're under stress, facing a deadline, or when things don't go your way. Do you get angry, annoyed, and frustrated, or anxious, worried, and ashamed? Maybe you shut down and get cold or unemotional, or hyper-focused and intense. There are countless responses, so take your time.

1. What are the three emotions you feel under stress or pressure (i.e., when you're in your Drama Mode)?

2. Pick one or more of the common Drama Modes from the table above or, better yet, come up with your own Drama Mode name. Get creative. It's helpful to pick a name that instantly reminds you that you really, really don't want to be that person.

Have patience with yourself if your Drama Mode appears more often than you'd like. It's a process to break out of old habits so we can form new, more empowering ones. In the next chapter, I'll show you how to become better at recognizing it, and better at quickly snapping out of it when it does come around.

CHAPTER 7

YOUR DRAMA CYCLE™

Your Drama Mode™ can activate the Drama Cycle™. The Drama Cycle starts with an external stimulus: a memory, an event, or something somebody says or does that launches your Drama Mode into action. You immediately and unconsciously focus on your external trigger, but you are often unaware of your thoughts at that moment because they arrive in milliseconds. What you are aware of is how you feel: shallow breathing, tense shoulders, butterflies in your stomach, heaviness in your chest, shortness of breath, etc. Sometimes we're not conscious of how we feel, physically, but our subconscious mind is acutely aware, using its tools from the past to stop the negative physical sensations. We retreat to our emotional comfort zone, and sometimes this means we react poorly in stressful situations.

Remember, we'll do just about anything to feel good. If we're feeling bad, we'll act instinctively and quickly to stop the negative feeling. This response happens so fast that our Drama Mode can seemingly come out of nowhere.

To consistently show up at your best, you need to identify and stop that cycle early. I'm not saying you should just clam up and swallow your feelings when someone's acting like a jerk. What I am saying is that you can learn to be more conscious and mindful about how you respond to jerks in general. You can choose not to be triggered!

Once you identify your triggers, you can practice new actions that break the cycle. You break the Drama Cycle by catching it the moment you begin to feel it in your body as tension or uneasiness. When you get better at noticing that moment, you will be more equipped to change your thoughts, and you can start understanding some of your old blind spots. Noticing what's happening in your body, then shifting your physical state to feel better in the moment, is how you begin to break through old patterns and shift your mindset!

Close-Up on the Drama Cycle™

Laura, Tony, and I each learned to spot events and experiences that were likely to trigger us and send us into a Drama Cycle.

- Tony's most common trigger was a call from a family member or an employee telling him that something wasn't going as planned.

- Laura was triggered by deadlines.

- I was often triggered by people disagreeing with me or approaching me in a way that I perceived as negative or discouraging.

Each of us knew we had a range of triggers and worked first on identifying our most common ones. We learned to spot them, and with practice, we learned to respond differently to them. You can learn to spot your triggers, too.

Tony's Drama Cycle

Here is Tony's Drama Cycle. Notice it begins with an external stimulus and then moves through what he focuses on, his thoughts, his physiological response, and his actions.

TONY'S DRAMA CYCLE™

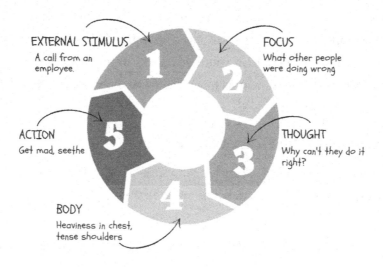

EXTERNAL STIMULUS
A call from an employee.

FOCUS
What other people were doing wrong

THOUGHT
Why can't they do it right?

BODY
Heaviness in chest, tense shoulders

ACTION
Get mad, seethe

1. **External stimulus.** The Drama Cycle starts with an external stimulus that triggers you into your Drama Mode. For Tony, it was usually a call or text from one of his employees about something Tony perceived as a problem.

2. **Focus.** When the external stimulus arises, your focus narrows. Tony focused on other people and on what he believed they were doing wrong. He focused on worries about the future, and the many ways things could go wrong.

3. **Thought.** Your focus leads almost instantly to a limiting thought. This happens so quickly that you may not even be conscious of it. Tony would automatically think, "Why can't these people do it right?"

4. **Body.** Your thoughts drive your body's response, and this may be the first thing you actually notice. You start feeling discomfort somewhere in your body; you do what it takes to get rid of the negative feeling. Tony felt a strong tension in his shoulders and a heaviness in his chest. In his case, it presented as an anxious feeling.

5. **Action**. At this point, you need to get rid of the bad feeling in your body. Tony was short with his employees to try to get them off the phone quickly and minimize his own negative feelings. But this didn't eliminate his discomfort. He would replay the interaction in his head for hours. What does your Drama Cycle look like? Use the following diagram to figure it out.

YOUR DRAMA CYCLE™

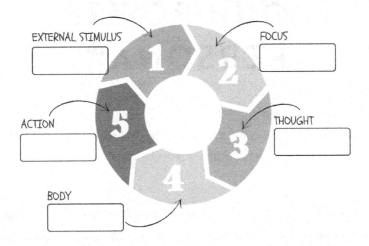

At this stage, people typically ask me one of the following questions:

- Now that I know what the Drama Cycle™ looks like, how do I get out of it?

- How do I snap out of my negative emotion in the moment when I am triggered?

- How do I move beyond all the drama when someone's not being nice or when they're in their Drama Mode™?

You'll begin to get the answers to those important questions in the next couple of chapters.

CHAPTER 8

YOUR POWER PERSONA™

"Every day think as you wake up, today I am fortunate to be alive. I have a precious human life. I am not going to waste it."

—*The Dalai Lama*

You can learn to outwit your Drama Mode. It happens when you make a conscious decision about who you want to be instead. The good news is you can be that person any time you choose.

Think of a day when you were clear-headed and energetic. When you walked out of an important meeting and said to yourself, "I nailed it!" The kind of day when you felt like you could take on the world. That's who you really are in your heart and soul, and it's the real you.

The real you is centered and full of positive energy, focused on serving something bigger than yourself. That's your Power Persona—and just like the Drama Mode, we all have one.

Your Power Persona is your true essence, without ego or pretense. It has nothing to prove because it's confident, and from that confidence comes humility. When you are in your Power Persona, you feel a deep sense of peace. You reach your highest level of consciousness, and because of that, you're able to accept what happens in each moment and address it from a place of gratitude and generosity. Where the Drama Mode is focused on fear and lack, the Power Persona is focused on what you can control in the moment. When you are in your Power Persona, you're showing up at your best. When you are consistently showing up at your best, you have influence over how you act (and react), and how you make other people feel. That's when you inspire others, and it's when you emerge as a leader in your own life.

If Our Power Persona Is the Real Us, Then Why Do We Have to Become It?

Because our Drama Mode is led by our ego, and it wants to be in charge. It's stubborn and it has learned to muscle its way into our everyday lives and bully our Power Persona into submission so it can meet its needs in the moment. Our Drama Mode's power comes from our limiting beliefs, rules, and judgments, and it likes when we rush through life without taking time to pause and reflect.

When we become conscious of what's happening in the moment, we give our Power Persona strength. At first this feels uncomfortable, but it gets easier with time and the more you practice embodying your Power Persona, the more natural it feels. Like you are seeing an old friend that you vaguely remember. At first you aren't comfortable with each other because it's been so long, but after a while, it's like no time has passed. Embodying your Power Persona liberates you from your ego and from the feeling of unease that accompanies the Drama Mode.

Notice that while you're not even aware when your Drama Mode takes over, your Power Persona assumes control as a matter of conscious choice. Your Power Persona is who you really are when you're at your best. It takes some work to find, name, and recognize, but the effort is worth it. Embodying your Power Persona will lead to your breakthrough moments. Those moments are waiting for you.

Let's Meet Some Power Personas

Tony and Tom Brady

When I asked Tony who he wanted to be instead of Uncle Pauley, he didn't hesitate. He said, "Tom Brady, and here's why:

"Tom Brady doesn't make excuses. He finds solutions, and he puts the work in. He's relentlessly positive. He looks for the good in people he works with, and together they find a way to deal constructively with whatever situation they find themselves in."

As he spoke to me about Tom Brady, Tony's body language and facial expression changed. Before, he had been slumped over slightly, and his features had shown stress. Now, as he started ticking off the ways in which, on his very best day, he followed the example of the future NFL Hall of Famer, he sat up straighter, and his eyes took on an air of purpose that I hadn't seen before.

From that moment on, things started to change for Tony. He got better at recognizing Uncle Pauley, and when he felt him trying to take command, he worked hard to change his approach, to match his Power Persona, Tom Brady. He started investing the time, attention, and resources to train his people–because, as he put it, "Tom Brady is all about accountability."

The transformation was astonishing, and it had a powerful impact, not only on his employees but on all his relationships. It was because of who started showing up for work each morning. Wouldn't your relationships improve if Tom Brady started showing up in all the places where Uncle Pauley had been making life miserable?

Before he identified his Power Persona, Tony had shown up as anxious, judgmental, and angry. After he identified and started living as his Power Persona, he showed up as energized, supportive, and focused. When Tony went from Uncle Pauley to Tom Brady, he changed his mantra from, "What the hell is wrong with these people?" to "How can I help them?" and "Let me find out what motivates them."

Although Tony has transformed his life, he still has many moments when he falls back into his old patterns. The difference though, is that now he has the tools to shift himself out of his Drama Mode faster so he can regain control of his life and become his Power Persona.

Laura and the Humanator

Laura's transformation culminated in her identifying not just Sharbie, but a Power Persona she called *The Humanator*, which was the opposite of her Drama Mode. The Humanator takes the relentless energy of Arnold Schwarzenegger's Terminator character and focuses that energy on being human and relating with other humans, instead of being a disconnected Barbie Doll. The Humanator connects deeply with people and is real with them. The Humanator is vulnerable and open about what she needs.

Laura's path was much different than Tony's, and that's OK. Some people take longer to identify and move away from their Drama Mode than others. The point is not to win a race, but to commit to doing the work to grow. Laura began the process by thinking about what requests she needed to turn down or delegate to create better boundaries in her life. This was challenging for her, because she had historically tied her self-worth to getting things done and feeling like people could rely on her.

She was eager to spend more time doing things that really mattered to her, and to be more strategic at work. She was missing so much because of her need for approval and her need to be in constant motion. Becoming the Humanator would help her connect with people as a real, imperfect human being, instead of showing up as a "perfect," plastic version of herself.

With patience and practice, Laura learned to recognize Sharbie whenever she showed up, and to replace her with the Humanator. Once she got the hang of shifting out of her Drama Mode, she began to see positive changes in her life. She learned how to communicate more clearly, set boundaries, and say no more. In turn, she had more energy to be there for the people who mattered most to her. She became less resentful and had more balance in her life.

Amal and the Dalai Lama

It took me much longer than I expected to choose my Power Persona. I kept gravitating toward highly successful people with qualities like passion and charisma. Although I admire those qualities, something felt off when I thought about choosing them for my Power Persona. It finally dawned on me that the attributes that would have the strongest countereffect to the Lash-Out Lunatic were quieter and less animated attributes like peace, joy, compassion, and love.

That's when I remembered the Dalai Lama. My immediate thought was, *Those attributes are boring and wimpy and choosing a Power Persona like the Dalai Lama would be corny.* But I eventually realized that was my Drama Mode talking. I was petrified about being vulnerable in any way. I had convinced myself that vulnerability was the same thing as weakness, when the truth is that real strength can only be found in vulnerability.

I researched the Dalai Lama and watched hours and hours of him speaking and teaching people about peace, love, and kindness. I found that he has a quiet strength and an amazing sense of humor. His presence has a profound calming effect on people. That's when I knew the Dalai Lama was indeed the perfect choice for my Power Persona.

- Where the Lash-Out Lunatic can be judgmental and even aggressive, the Dalai Lama is kind and compassionate.

- Where the Lash-Out Lunatic can be harsh and negative toward others, the Dalai Lama is positive and optimistic, and makes a habit of seeing the best in people, and assuming the best about them.

- Where the Lash-Out Lunatic has a way of flying off the handle and reacting heedlessly and without thought or consideration to people and events, the Dalai Lama is calm and grounded.

A Power Persona List

Power Personas are the opposite of Drama Modes. Your Power Persona should embody the emotions you want to feel and the qualities you want to have.

Here is a short list of people with admirable qualities to get you to start thinking about who you want your Power Persona to be. This list is provided only to get your imagination working; you don't have to choose one from the list. In fact, it's best if you come up with your own. Your Power Persona doesn't have to resemble anyone. What matters is that it includes the attributes you admire most.

- Super Hero (strong/steady/secure)
- Mother Theresa (compassionate/giving/peaceful)
- Serena Williams (powerful/vibrant/feminine)
- Malala Yousafzai (brave/determined/compassionate)
- Oprah Winfrey (courageous/purposeful/grounded)
- Dalai Lama (compassionate/joyful/peaceful)
- Michael Jordan (dynamic/energetic/tenacious)
- Martin Luther King (influential/dynamic/inspiring)
- Nelson Mandela (inspiring/brave/peaceful)
- Toni Morrison (creative/honest/inspired)
- Leonardo Da Vinci (brilliant/curious/creative)
- Mohammad Ali (confident/determined/magnetic)
- Rosa Parks (groundbreaking/inspiring/brave)
- Buddha (calm/centered/enlightened)
- Socrates (wise/industrious/calm)

EXERCISE: Choosing Your Power Persona

Take some time right now to think about your Power Persona.

When you think about your Power Persona, think about the opposite of your Drama Mode. Who do you want to be instead? Who are you in your heart and soul when you are at peace, energetic, compassionate, and strong? The most important thing is that your Power Persona has meaning to you.

1. What are the three emotions you feel when you're at your best (which are often the opposite of those you feel when you're in your Drama Mode)? List them here:

2. Think about a person you admire. What three qualities do they have that you wish you had? Write them here:

3. Choose a name for your Power Persona based on your answers to questions one and two. It could be a real person from any time, a fictional character, or a made-up name.

4. Now, let's come up with a mantra (or two) for your Power Persona. Let's say you chose Socrates, for his wisdom and calm. Your mantra might be, "I love challenges; they invigorate me."

Take some time to identify the right words before you decide your new mantras. You have years of practice with your old negative thoughts. You must practice replacing them with new thoughts that focus on something you can control, and that will encourage your forward momentum. Generally, your new mantras should help you defuse the ones you repeat when you're in your Drama Mode.

CHAPTER 9

THE POWER CYCLE

*"The greatest glory in living lies not in never falling,
but in rising every time we fall."*

—*Nelson Mandela*

Power Cycle Definition:

The tool you use to short-circuit your Drama Cycle, so you can shift your mindset the moment you're triggered and become your Power Persona.

What determines how we feel at any moment in time? Is it what's happening externally? Other people's bad behavior, the economy, or the weather? Of course, these things have an impact on how we feel, but our emotions at any particular moment are a result of how we direct our mind and body. No matter what's happening in our lives, we are in control of our own emotional state. Once we believe that and learn how to shift our mindset, we have direct control over our level of energy and happiness.

Based on what you've learned about the Drama Cycle, you know that when you're feeling a negative emotion like anger, frustration, anxiety, or fear, you're most likely repeating an old story in your head. How do you snap out of it?

I could tell you to change your story – to change what you repeat to yourself and what you're focused on, but that won't do much to change how you feel in the moment. It will just seem like positive thinking. Your heart rate has already started racing, your shoulders have tightened, and at this point shifting your brain's focus can only do so much. In a sense you're hypnotizing yourself by repeating your mantras until you believe them. What you focus on does matter, and what you repeat to yourself will lead to your results, BUT simply changing your mantras and focus won't do much to change in the moment you're feeling triggered. There's only one way to change your emotions on a visceral level vs. intellectually or superficially, and that is to make a physiological change.

Our physical and emotional states are tightly linked. Let's say you think you're going to lose your job because you made a mistake at work. Most likely, you won't lose your job, but your brain begins to focus on all the things that could happen if you did. You think about how long it would take for you to get another good paying job and how difficult it would be to pay your bills. Before you know it, your palms are sweating, your heart is beating faster, and you have a lump in your throat. Your cortisol levels begin to surge, which makes you feel even more stressed.

See how your thoughts can trigger a physical response? Once you start having a physical reaction, changing your thoughts doesn't do much to reduce the cortisol coursing through your body. The quickest way to change how you feel at that moment is to do something physical to snap yourself out of it.

Tap Into the Power of Your Body

Some of my clients begin by resisting the idea that we can control our emotions, until they experience it for themselves. My client Peter and I were having a coaching session after he'd had a big fight with his wife. He was thinking about all the things that were going wrong in his marriage and was picturing what his life would be like if they broke up. He was focused on all the ways she was being unreasonable, and he couldn't see how they would get past this. I had never heard him sound that way, his energy was low, he was speaking quietly and seemed hopeless. He kept talking about all the negative things that could happen – he was deeply entrenched in his Drama Cycle.

We talked for a while, but nothing I said at that moment was going to get him to focus on what he could control, so I told him to get his sneakers on. "What?" Peter said, sounding surprised. I said, "Get your sneakers on now as we're talking, I want you to go for a one-mile run." "I'm not doing that; I don't feel like it. Don't you understand, Amal, my marriage might end." "Peter, please get your sneakers on," I said. "But I haven't run in forever," he said. "Then walk or jog, I don't care but you need to do this." We went back and forth for a while until he realized I wasn't going to back down. He put his sneakers on and walked out the door before we hung up. "Another thing," I said, "I want you to tell yourself that you're a superhero while you run." (his Power Persona) I'm sure he rolled his eyes, but he knew me by now, so he didn't argue. Twenty minutes later he sent me video of himself running and yelling, I fu**ing, am a Superhero!"

He sent me the following text two days later: "I can't thank you enough for snapping me out of it the other day and getting my head out of my ass so I can see things a lot more clearly. I don't know what I would have done without you. I went for another run yesterday – starting to get a little bit more momentum. One day at a time. Thank you, thank you, thank you!"

The best part of the story is that Peter was able to communicate with his wife more productively when he got out of the Drama Cycle, and they're still happily married.

You have power over how you feel!

The secret to shifting out of the Drama Cycle is to use physical energy to change your emotional state. Amy Cuddy is a social psychologist who proved that you can change your biochemistry by changing how you move your body. In a study she did at Harvard University in 2010, she proved that practicing power poses for only two minutes decreased cortisol (the stress hormone) by 25% and increased testosterone (the hormone connected with feeling confident) by 19%. Take a few minutes to look her up on YouTube and watch her powerful TED talk on this extraordinary physiological phenomenon... and you will be inspired to harness the power of your physical body, too.[12]

EXERCISE: The Power Cycle

Again, just being conscious of your behavior isn't enough to change it. The quickest and most effective way to snap yourself out of your Drama Mode is to change your physical state in the moment you feel the most stress. The Power Cycle is a powerful tool to help you shift your physical energy quickly. Whenever you notice yourself feeling anxious, frustrated, or angry with someone or about a situation, use The Power Cycle to snap out of it. The power of this tool is in its simplicity.

Tony's Power Cycle

When Tony got a call from an employee with a problem, he learned to become aware of a rising tension in his chest and a tightness in his shoulders. At that moment, he entered the Power Cycle by shifting his physical energy. Once he shifted his physical state, it felt easier to shift his emotional state. While taking a few deep breaths, he relaxed his shoulders, then put a big smile on his face and said his new mantra to himself, "It's not their fault. I will train them." At first, he felt self-conscious, like he was faking, and he was worried people would think something was wrong with him. No one seemed to notice though, and he was surprised at how quickly those deep breaths and that smile changed the way he felt. He decided to practice The Power Cycle whenever he got annoyed, which was a lot. Before he knew it, he started breathing and smiling without having to think about it. He told me later that using this simple tool made a huge positive impact in his life. It allowed him to step back and focus on the things that were most important to him. He took time to think about the kind of leader he wanted to be and decided that he was passionate about helping people grow so they could experience their own transformations. His purpose, he realized, was to continually grow as a person and to help others be their best.

TONY'S POWER CYCLE™
✱ NOTICE BODY & FOCUS SWITCH

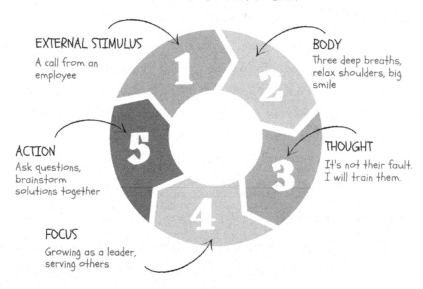

EXTERNAL STIMULUS
A call from an employee

BODY
Three deep breaths, relax shoulders, big smile

ACTION
Ask questions, brainstorm solutions together

THOUGHT
It's not their fault. I will train them.

FOCUS
Growing as a leader, serving others

1. **External stimulus.** The Power Cycle begins with the same external stimulus as the Drama Cycle. For Tony it was a call or text from one of his employees about something he would have perceived as a problem when he was in his Drama Mode.

2. **Body**. Notice that in your Power Cycle, step two becomes Body, because as you now know, that's where you need to start to shift your state. Once you shift your physical state, you can consciously choose a thought and your focus will follow. In Tony's Drama Mode, he immediately felt a heaviness in his chest and tension in his body. To counteract that feeling, he now takes three deep breaths, relaxes his shoulders, and puts a big smile on his face.

3. Thought. As you are shifting your physical state by doing something different with your body, you consciously choose a new, empowering mantra to replace the negative one in your Drama Cycle. Tony's mantra in his Power Cycle is, "It's not their fault. I will train them." In your Power Cycle, you are no longer a slave to your subconscious patterns, instead you consciously decide how you want to feel instead.

4. Focus. When you're in your Power Cycle, you expand your focus to include the things that are most important to you, your values and purpose. In his Drama Cycle, Tony focused on other people and on what he believed they were doing wrong, as well as worries about the future. In his Power Cycle, he focused on how he could make a difference in the world by serving people and helping them grow. You may notice that when people are in their Drama Cycle, they focus on what they aren't getting, and when people are in the Power Cycle, they focus on what they can give.

5. Action. When you are in your Power Cycle, you choose the action you take. Before, Tony responded to his triggers the only way he knew how, using the tools he learned from his Map. Back then, he focused on removing any discomfort or anxiety he was feeling; it was a reaction that seemed to come out of nowhere. He was short with his employees, then would replay the interaction in his head for hours. Now, he is conscious about the way he responds. He takes time to understand the problem and asks questions about how he can help. Because he's focused on the bigger picture, on his purpose of continual growth and supporting others, he shows up with a different kind of energy.

You now have the POWER to focus your attention on the solution, rather than the problem. The Power Cycle helps you snap you out of the Drama Cycle. It does that by harnessing the power of your physiology, so you can consciously direct your mind where you want it to go. We may think we're powerless to change our thoughts, but The Power Cycle proves we can. It seems simple, too simple to work, but it works because it's so simple! You can control your mind by changing your physical state. When you can master this in the most challenging moments then you become an expert at shifting your mindset.

Don't just read about it. Do it!

Commit to identifying what you will do physically to shift your mindset in the moment, as well as what your new, positive mantra will be. Then practice The Power Cycle before you move on to the next chapter. By committing to this and practicing it when you notice yourself slipping into your Drama Mode, you will take control of your emotions. Remember, whatever you focus on, you create more of. Make sure you're creating more of what you want in your life!

What does your Power Cycle Look Like? Fill in the diagram below, using Tony's completed worksheet as a guide, and find out right now. Make sure your responses reflect your own experience.

YOUR POWER CYCLE™
✳ NOTICE BODY & FOCUS SWITCH

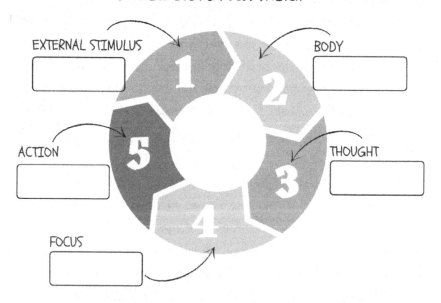

CHAPTER 10

SHIFTING FROM DRAMA MODE TO POWER PERSONA

"If you do what you've always done, you'll get what you've always gotten."

—Anonymous

For most of us, it takes time, patience, and support to identify our Drama Mode and replace it with a transformative Power Persona. Here are four simple steps that will help you make it happen:

Step 1: Analyze what's going on emotionally when you go into your Drama Mode.

What are the three emotions or responses you typically feel when you're in your Drama Mode? For Tony and me, the common emotions were fear, anger, and anxiety. For Laura, her responses were anxiety, frustration, and shutdown.

What are the three emotions or responses you notice when you are in your Drama Mode?

1.

2.

3.

What emotions do you want to consistently feel in your life ... to replace the emotions you feel when you are in your Drama Mode?

1.

2.

3.

These should be the opposite of the emotions you feel in your Drama Mode and should be at the heart of your Power Persona. For example, Laura felt anxious, frustrated, and angry when she was Sharbie, so she chose a Power Persona that would feel peaceful, accepting, and happy. She practiced using The Power Cycle to shift out of her Drama Mode, and after a while was able to embody the Humanator and feel more positive emotions.

Step 2: Analyze what's going on in your body right before you go into your Drama Mode.

Again, you may first become aware of the physical sensation before you become aware of what you're saying to yourself. Get clear about what's happening in your body when your trigger shows up by asking yourself where in your body you feel those emotions. In my case, I felt tightness in my chest and shortness of breath.

It's important to identify how you feel physically when you're in your Drama Mode because the way out of the Drama Cycle starts by harnessing the power of your physical energy. We have a strong drive to stop negative physical sensations and will sometimes use old, limiting patterns to stop those feelings. The Power Cycle helps you become consciously aware of how you're feeling physically so you can choose a more productive response. When I begin to feel that familiar tightness in my chest, I take a few deep belly breaths, and relax my shoulders, which immediately helps me shift my energy.

What do you feel in your body when you go into the Drama Cycle?

1.

2.

3.

What will you do to shift your physical state the moment you feel triggered?

1.

2.

3.

Step 3: Ask yourself WHY your Drama Mode shows up.

Nine times out of ten, one or more of our three emotional needs trigger our Drama Mode: the need to feel connected, safe, and worthy. The reason we created our Map in the first place is to satisfy these needs. We can also go into our Drama Mode for a variety of other reasons that aren't as deep. These can include when we're tired, hungry, craving more balance or attention, or when we've been avoiding something. Recognizing these triggers is an important step to shifting your mindset.

What need most commonly triggers your Drama Mode? The need to feel a sense of control when your world seems out of control, the need to feel validated and appreciated, or the need to connect with others or to be part of a group?

Is there another pattern or trigger you notice? If so, what is it?

Step 4: What are the most common mantras you repeat when you're in your Drama Mode?

1.

2.

3.

What new, empowering mantras will you choose to replace the negative ones in your Drama Cycle?

1.

2.

3.

Be patient with yourself when you begin using The Power Cycle. It's common for our Drama Mode to get the best of us at times, but if you consistently practice The Power Cycle, you'll be amazed at how much control you have. After a while, you'll build momentum, and that's when you'll feel more confident and energized by the process.

CHAPTER 11

WHAT TO DO WHEN SOMEONE ELSE GOES INTO THEIR DRAMA MODE

There will be times when you get frustrated because it feels like you're doing all the hard work to show up at your best, and other people aren't meeting you halfway. It would be easy to stay in your Power Persona if it weren't for other people!

So, what should you do when you feel like you're about to get triggered by someone else's drama? Practice the three steps to shifting your mindset.

Step One: Focus on what you can control.

There are two things you have complete control over: your thoughts and your actions. You have influence over other things, but no real control. When you're in your Power Persona, you don't waste energy complaining about how someone else is showing up, instead you consciously focus on what you're thinking and what you're doing. Most people are continually keeping score, at least subconsciously. We're more focused on what the other person is doing wrong and how it's impacting us, than on what we're doing or how we can help them to be better. When you shift your focus away from what you're not getting, you free yourself from your own Drama Mode. This shift in mindset is the single most powerful tool my clients practice to become better leaders.

In her book, *This Isn't the Life I Ordered*, Jenniffer Weigel says, "Everyone who is mean is one deep breath away from tears, we have to love them all."[13] OK, maybe you don't have to love them, but thinking this thought could get you a step closer to having compassion for them. I know it's easier said than done to be the bigger person, but I promise you, it gets easier with practice.

Step Two: Remember it's not you!

The best way to approach someone who's in their Drama Mode is to take a step back and think about why they're acting that way. Often, we take offense to someone else's behavior when it has nothing to do with us. People act out when they feel pain – and anxiety and fear are the most common reasons for that pain. They may feel overwhelmed or frustrated, and the only way they know how to respond is the way they always have, the way they learned because of their Map.

Once you've done the work to uncover your own Drama Mode, you'll have more empathy for others when they're in theirs. When you can see the situation rationally, without your own emotional baggage in the way, you understand that people go into their Drama Mode when they feel like they're losing control or when they feel insignificant. This understanding will help you focus on the actions you can take to guide others to meet their needs in more productive ways.

Approaching someone with compassion and understanding has a disarming effect. It helps you rise above the conflict, puts their guard down, and makes them more open to understanding you (and themselves) better.

Step Three: Serve something bigger than yourself

Several years ago, I read a book that changed my life. It's called *The Go-Giver: A Little Story About a Powerful Business Idea*, by Bob Burg and

John David Mann. It's a fable about a young salesperson named Joe who prided himself on doing what it took to make the sale. The book takes us on his journey from being a go-getter to becoming a go-giver. He learned that he could achieve greater results in the long run by shifting his focus from what he could get from other people to what he could give to them. He put "The Five Laws of Stratospheric Success" into practice and began seeing amazing results in all areas of his life.[14]

The Five Laws of Stratospheric Success, The Go-Giver, Bob Burg

The Law of Value:

Your true worth is determined by how much more you give in value than you take in payment.

The Law of Compensation:

Your income is determined by how many people you serve and how well you serve them.

The Law of Influence:

Your influence is determined by how abundantly you place other people's interest first.

The Law of Authenticity:

The most valuable gift you have to offer is yourself.

The Law of Receptivity:

The key to effective giving is to stay open to receiving.

The reason this book resonated with me so much was because I had always been a go-getter. I valued achievement and all the grit, tenacity and sacrifice associated with it. Like many of my high achieving clients, I thought I needed to compete to get a piece of the pie. This book helped me see that the pie is big enough for everyone, and that when we add value and approach people with honesty and understanding, their natural inclination is to reciprocate.

It's funny how the universe works. Within days of reading this book I got a call to participate in a project for a consulting company. The goal of the project was to research the best leaders and companies of all time and identify the things that led to their success. These companies were the best in their industries, and they succeeded when others had failed, even in down economies. There were several things they did well, but one thing kept coming up, again and again: they served instead of sold.

Dutch Bros. Example

One company on the list was Dutch Bros. Coffee, founded by brothers Travis and Dane Boersma in Grants Pass, Ore., in 1992. Dutch Bros is the largest privately owned drive-through coffee company in the United States. Travis and Dane started out with one pushcart that they parked by the railroad tracks in Grants Pass. They blasted their favorite music and experimented with different coffee drinks, giving away many of their creations.[15] Dutch Bros now has more than 300 locations in the U.S. and is still growing. Although they serve quality coffee, their purpose goes beyond their product. Both Travis and Dane had a vision to make a positive difference in people's lives. They sold coffee but their mission was to spread love.

Dane passed away in 2009 from ALS. Since then, Travis has upheld the mission and honored his brother's memory by exemplifying the qualities that helped them gain success in the early years. Here's Travis's mission statement:

"I, Travis Boersma, see, hear, and know that the purpose of my life is to enjoy the journey, to maximize the moment, to be a loving, passionate, inspirational leader that defies the odds, to be a force for God and a force for good. I hope to meet the man that I am someday when I die, not the man that I could have been."[16]

In an interview in 2019, Travis said that his vision is to impact the communities his company serves. "Through the Dutch Bros Foundation and local franchisees, Dutch Bros donates several million dollars to support its customers, local communities and nonprofit organizations."[17]

I love this example because Travis Boersma practices what he preaches. His company is successful, but he's driven by more than money. It's obvious he cares about people and wants to make a positive impact in the world. Who wouldn't want a boss like that?

This research affirmed what I was seeing with my clients.

I began having each client read *The Go-Giver* and put the principles into practice in their own lives. Remarkable things were happening: one client finally closed a big deal she had been working on for over three years, another got two promotions in two years. Many people just felt better: less stressed, and more confident.

When you give without thinking about what people will give back to you, you get back tenfold.

This works in your personal life as well. If you have a partner in your life, you can try an assignment I sometimes give my clients. For the next two weeks, go above and beyond for them, do nice things, and give more time and attention than you usually would. Do all this without expecting anything in return. Here's what's going to happen: They're going to ask you what you want, because they're not used to people operating this way. Even if you have a good relationship, you're human, which means you have a tally going somewhere in the back of your mind when it comes to your relationship.

I'll be honest, the first several times I tried this exercise with my husband Jimmy, I couldn't get past day three, because I kept thinking, "I'm doing all these nice things and he's not reciprocating." I wasn't doing these good deeds from my heart, but because I wanted something in return. That mindset was coming from insecurity and fear. When I finally let go and got over my fear of being vulnerable, things changed for the better. I focused on all Jimmy's good attributes and reminded myself to assume positive intent. The more vulnerable I was, the more vulnerable he became. That's because energy is reciprocal: when I put out positive energy, that's what I got back.

Once you get in the habit of giving, you'll need to be prepared for an avalanche of generosity from others. It's important to stay open to receiving, which is often a challenge for people. We're taught from a very young age that it's better to give than to receive, so sometimes receiving brings up discomfort. If that happens, practice being present in the moment and acknowledging the feeling, so you can release it. You may have to remind yourself that receiving is a natural part of the cycle of giving; if you remove that step, the cycle breaks down. You deserve to receive abundance in your life.

Also, giving to others starts with giving to yourself. If you're depleting your energy to be there for everyone else, sooner or later you burn yourself out and feel resentful. This can happen even if you have the best intentions. So, giving doesn't mean always saying yes. It means prioritizing the things that matter most and learning how to set boundaries. When you do this, you'll say yes when you really mean it, and you'll show up with an open heart. People will know they can rely on you, and they will respect you more because of it. This is a great way to build confidence.

The Three Steps in Action

When I met my client Suzanne, she was spending a lot of energy feeling frustrated with her boss Patrick. Patrick was the founder and CEO of a software company, and Suzanne was the head of HR. Patrick had many good qualities, including vision, tenacity, and passion. He also had a few blind spots that triggered Suzanne: he was opinionated, and he often made rash decisions without having all the facts. Patrick blindsided her more than once with decisions that infuriated her and her team.

When I started working with Suzanne, she was so frustrated with Patrick that it was keeping her up at night. She spent our whole first session complaining about his faults and how unbearable he was to work with. She said, "I can't stand it anymore! He's completely clueless, and he has no respect for what my team and I do for this company. I'm not the only one who's annoyed either, the whole executive team is frustrated with him." I took a deep breath, "Let's focus on you for now. How do you know he doesn't respect you?" "Well, if he did, he wouldn't act this way." "Really? Are you sure about that? Have you talked to him about how you've been feeling?" Suzanne laughed sarcastically, "Yeah right, he won't listen, so why should I bother?"

A few things were happening that Suzanne wasn't aware of. First, she was making some big assumptions about what was going on in Patrick's mind and she was seeking evidence from other people about why she was right. Second, she was taking his actions personally. And third, she was spending her precious time and energy focusing on what was out of her control (Patrick's thoughts and actions) instead of what was within her control (her own thoughts and actions).

Suzanne was doing something so many of us do, she was making assumptions about what someone else, in this case, her boss, was thinking. She created a story in her head about how he would respond if she spoke openly with him about the way she was feeling. This was a limiting belief that came from her own Map: Suzanne was uncomfortable having difficult conversations, so it was easier to focus on how bad Patrick was to work with than to face her fear of approaching him directly. Since Suzanne wasn't open with Patrick, she didn't give him the opportunity to share his perspective or to learn from hers. Additionally, she took his behavior personally, when it had nothing to do with her. Patrick was operating from his own Map, one that was focused on his ability to get things done quickly and efficiently.

At our next session Suzanne and I continued our conversation about Patrick. "Suzanne, you've been reinforcing your belief that Patrick is unreasonable by seeking evidence to prove you're right. You've been spending a lot of time complaining about him with your colleagues on the executive team." She replied, "That's not true, you don't understand Amal, everybody agrees with me that he's been difficult." I said, "Let's do a little exercise." She sighed, a little annoyed, "OK, if you say so." "Take a couple minutes and look for everything in this room that's blue." She looked around slowly, paying close attention to everything she saw that was blue. "OK, now tell me everything you saw that was green." She laughed, "I honestly can't think of one thing, you told me to focus on blue things." Exactly, what you focus on, grows. If you're looking for blue things, that's what you'll find; there are lots of green things right there in front of you, but you don't even notice them.

Suzanne's Options

I told Suzanne she had three options:

1. Keep doing what you've been doing.

2. Talk to Patrick about how you're feeling.

3. Leave the company.

If Suzanne stayed and did nothing, she would continue to feel frustrated, she would continue to lose sleep, and her stress level would get worse. She said, "That's not an option. If things continue the way they have been, I don't know what will happen, but it won't be good." Suzanne knew she could find another job, but she liked the people she worked with, and she really wanted to find a way to stay, so she made the decision to talk with Patrick. "The idea of talking to Patrick makes me nervous," Suzanne said. "I really don't think he has the capacity to hear me." I said, "If you go into a conversation with that mindset, then you'll get negative results. You get what you expect, and besides, what do you have to lose at this point? Remember your other two options." "That's true, but this makes me really uncomfortable," Suzanne replied. "It would be strange if it didn't, Suzanne. The more you act when you're uncomfortable, the easier it will get. Think of it this way, you're giving this situation the respect it deserves. By having this conversation, you have the capacity to influence Patrick positively, and in turn make a positive impact on the entire company. That's true leadership."

Suzanne spent the next couple weeks learning how to have a difficult conversation. She practiced how to speak honestly and openly, in a way that wouldn't make Patrick feel defensive, then she scheduled the conversation. Patrick reacted much better than she thought he would. He was surprised at how frustrated she had been feeling and he apologized. He admitted that he had been feeling stressed because the company missed their last financial target, and the Board of Directors was putting pressure on him. She apologized because she hadn't come to him earlier. Suzanne was relieved and pleased at how well the conversation went.

I told Suzanne that this conversation was an important step, but it was only the beginning. If she wanted to change the way she was feeling and to make a bigger impact at work, she would need to continue to practice the three steps to shifting her mindset, and she would need to get in the habit of communicating what she was feeling. She committed to doing what it took to feel more confident and less stressed.

When I checked in with Suzanne three months later, she seemed like a different person. She had gotten so good at having difficult conversations that other members of the executive team asked her to teach them how to do it. She admitted that Patrick still made her feel frustrated at times, but she didn't allow herself to stay there for long. She made a commitment to deal with issues as they came up and to communicate openly about how she felt. "Sometimes he sees my point of view and sometimes he doesn't, but at least now I feel like we're having more productive conversations and I have more control over the outcome. I understand that he has a Map just like I do, and he's meeting his needs the best way he knows how." I laughed because she sounded just like me. I left our meeting feeling good because I could tell Suzanne's mindset made her feel happier.

It's Your Turn

The next time you feel frustrated by someone, use these three steps:

Step One: Focus on what you can control.

Step Two: Remember, it's not you!

Step Three: Serve something bigger than yourself.

Practicing the steps may feel uncomfortable at first, but it will get easier each time you do it. If you commit to making the three steps part of your daily life, you'll start to feel more relaxed overall and less triggered by others. You'll be better able to step away from tough situations and focus on the bigger picture. You'll see people respond to you more positively, and they'll want to be around you because they will want to feel the same way you do.

EXERCISE: Practice the Three Steps Yourself

Whenever my clients complain about someone else, I have them go on a fact-finding mission so they can better understand that person's Map. When you know why someone is acting in a certain way, then you have a better chance of connecting with them and helping them meet their needs more effectively.

1. Get curious about their Map. How do they meet their three emotional needs? (The need to feel secure, worthy, and connected)

2. Look for the good, seek evidence about their positive qualities and intentions.

3. Focus on what you can control, (your thoughts and your actions) and communicate your needs in a productive way.

4. Think of one or two ways you can help them reduce their stress level.

CHAPTER 12

HOW TO MAKE PEACE, VITALITY, AND HAPPINESS YOUR BASELINE EMOTIONS

"It's like a mother, when the baby is crying, she picks up the baby tenderly in her arms. Your pain, your anxiety is your baby. You have to take care of it. You have to go back to yourself, to recognize the suffering in you, embrace the suffering, and you get relief."

—*Thich Nhat Hanh*

We've talked a lot about how to snap out of the Drama Cycle in the moment, when you're triggered into your Drama Mode. In this chapter, I'll share the steps you can take to make deep peace, happiness, and vitality your baseline emotions. These positive emotions give you power to shift your mindset, so you can become your Power Persona. When you become who you are meant to be in your heart and soul, you feel complete, so things that would have made you feel anxious or frustrated before, don't have the same effect on you. You no longer feel burdened by fear and worry because you have faith that everything will be OK. This faith doesn't just pop out of thin air, though. It comes from a commitment to living your life on a deeper level and to serving something bigger than yourself. Here's how you will get there.

Remember Why You Have a Drama Mode

Remember, you developed your Drama Mode to meet one or more of your three emotional needs, to feel connected, secure, and worthy. As I mentioned earlier, we learned to meet these needs when we were young, the best way we could with the tools that were available to us at the time. These tools were rudimentary, so as we got older and our lives got more complicated, they couldn't keep up and often ended up hurting us more than they helped. For example, if you didn't feel secure as a child, you learned to protect yourself by keeping people at arm's length and by shielding your heart from pain. As you grew up, and people tried to connect with you, this old pattern kicked in. It kept people away to protect you, but it ended up making you feel isolated and lonely. We're wired to connect with other human beings, in fact sharing and connecting are important ways to feel secure.

It can feel uncomfortable to change old patterns because you've been using them for so long, and they've met your needs, even if only slightly. When you attempt to change the way you meet a need, you may feel exposed, and you may even feel some form of shame. That's because we're hard on ourselves. We have high expectations, and if we make a mistake, we don't give ourselves the grace we would give someone else.

There's nothing wrong with having these needs, they're a natural part of the human condition. It's how you meet them that matters.

Next time you catch an old pattern and start to feel bad, think of yourself as a child. Have the same compassion for yourself as you would have for a 5-year-old who's suffering now. The only way to set yourself free from old limiting patterns is to understand why you created them in the first place and to appreciate what you were trying to do to meet your needs. Then you can consciously create new, healthier patterns that serve you and everyone around you.

You Can't Truly Love Other People Until You Love Yourself

If you're still reading this book, it means you're serious about personal growth, and I would be willing to bet you finish what you start. You're probably an achiever. Most of us achievers are hard on ourselves. We feel the same emotions as everyone else, but we rarely allow ourselves to sit with those emotions, because we're too busy with all the things we want to do in our lives. When I say sit with our emotions, I don't mean to wallow in them. I mean to acknowledge them and feel them so we can release them.

I've always been hard on people, judging them over the littlest things. Since I judged myself so harshly, I held others to that same impossible standard. When I realized how much my judgment was keeping me from being the person I wanted to be, I worked on having more compassion for others. No matter how hard I tried to lighten up and let go, though, I couldn't seem to change. It took years for me to understand that I needed to start with myself.

Earlier, I told you about my Drama Mode, Sergeant Pain. When I'm in this Drama Mode, I say things like, "I need to snap out of it," and "What the hell is wrong with me?" As the name suggests, this Drama Mode causes me pain, it pushes me to swallow my feelings and to constantly strive for perfection. Since there's no such thing as perfection, it creates a perpetual sense of failure.

Becoming aware of Sergeant Pain was the first step to changing this old pattern. It's a work in progress, though. I still have moments where she wants to take control, but I'm learning to have more compassion for myself by paying attention to the things I say in my head. I've noticed that when

I allow myself to be a flawed person with human emotions, other people are more inclined to do the same. This has helped me connect more deeply with many people in my life.

If you have a high level of stress or anxiety, you may be hard on yourself, too. You may push yourself physically and emotionally like I did. You may distract yourself with constant activity, or focus on perfection, at the expense of your well-being.

When we're hard on ourselves, we're uncomfortable making mistakes. We want to be seen as smart and capable. That mindset sets us up for failure, though. Mistakes are necessary, in fact, they're important stepping stones to success. I love the famous quote by Thomas Edison, "I have not failed 10,000 times – I've successfully found 10,000 ways that won't work."[18] His perspective kept him open to learning from his mistakes. When you release the need to control what happens and how people perceive you, you stay receptive to gifts from the universe. Jack Canfield, coauthor of *Chicken Soup for the Soul*, says, "If you pay attention, you will realize that the universe is sending you signals all the time that show you where you need to go and what you need to do to create the life of your dreams."[19] I used to think this concept was too touchy- feely until I experienced the series of events I told you about in the beginning of the book. First, I blacked out while driving on the highway, then my mom died, then I got fired.

I had been working at a really stressful job for a few years before I briefly blacked out on the highway. For a long time, I had been walking around with a pit in my stomach and a heaviness in my chest. These feelings were clear signs that I needed to make changes in my life, but I ignored them. I was making too much money, and sales was all I knew how to do. Blacking out while driving was the first whisper from the universe, "You can't keep up like this, Amal. Listen to your body." Instead, I kept pushing forward, telling myself I would be fine. Sergeant Pain was running the show although I wasn't aware of it. I didn't even know how to care for myself at that point.

I got my second message from the universe after my mom died, and this time, it wasn't a whisper. Her death knocked the wind out of me. I felt lower than I ever had in my life, like a piece of me died with her. I had an emptiness I couldn't fill, and nothing made me happy. At the time, I didn't understand that this emptiness was a natural part of the mourning process. If I had slowed down and given myself the care I needed, I would have been able to experience the pain and move forward. But Sergeant Pain didn't allow me to feel my emotions, so I distracted myself with things that made me feel better in the moment. This only created more pain. I felt restless, and I began to daydream about leaving my husband and finding my "soulmate." Jimmy and I had been going through the motions in our marriage, focusing our time and energy on raising our kids and on making money. We were at a crossroads, we could either grow apart, or grow closer. My unhappiness was a big push from the universe to make a move. It eventually forced me to face what was broken in our marriage, and finally open up to him about my feelings.

This experience was a blessing. It prompted us to do the work we needed to do to create a solid, loving connection. Like all couples, we have our ups and downs, but now we're in a place where we have fun together and cherish each other.

Although the first two universal messages got my attention, the third one changed everything. As I mentioned earlier, after I blacked out at the wheel, I got a new sales job thinking it would make me feel less stressed and more fulfilled. About a year after starting at my new company I got fired. At first, I was devastated. I was embarrassed and emotional, I cried for two days. I worried about what people would think of me, then after a week or so, I shifted my focus to what I knew in my heart. The truth was my heart wasn't in that job from the beginning. I felt lighter, more at peace, and I could breathe easily for the first time in years. I don't think I would be where I am today if I hadn't gotten fired. It would have been too scary to walk away from the security of a weekly paycheck. I may not have answered my call to live my purpose, I wouldn't be in the position to help people, and I wouldn't be writing this book.

Learn to Surrender

I encourage my clients to focus on spiritual growth, knowing that spirituality means different things to different people. That means using their beliefs to deepen their connection with something greater than themselves, whether that's God, Buddha, humanity, nature, or the universe.

I tend to use God and the universe interchangeably but feel free to replace those words with what feels right to you. Being spiritual doesn't mean you have to adhere to a particular religion; it's more about living your life on a deeper level and being aware of how precious and fleeting it is. It's about finding a way to connect with what matters, so your life has more meaning, and you're not just going through the motions. As Pierre Teilhard de Chardin said, "We are spiritual beings, having a human experience." It's easy to forget this when we're caught up in the constant activity of our hectic lives. Then we wonder why we feel stressed out and dissatisfied.

I always valued achievement. If I had a goal, I would put all my energy into reaching it, getting up at 4 a.m. and working hard all day. I learned how to persist, to forgo fun and relaxation so I could get what I wanted. I was never satisfied, though. Once I reached a goal, instead of giving myself time to enjoy my accomplishment, I was on to the next one. I was so focused on results that my energy took on an almost manic quality. All that pushing and striving only intensified my perfectionist tendencies. I had financial success, but I wasn't happy. I tried many techniques to find peace. Nothing worked until I learned how to surrender.

My definition of surrendering is using the energy of the universe to achieve at the highest level by doing the work, then detaching from the outcome.

When you work hard toward your goals, then let go of the outcome, magical things happen. If you've ever baked bread, you're familiar with this concept: kneading the dough is important but allowing the dough time to rest and rise is equally important. Another example that comes to mind is the time Jimmy brought his prized tomato seeds home from his uncle's garden in Greece. His uncle's tomatoes were amazing: red, and juicy, and bursting with flavor. Jimmy was so excited to plant them in our garden that spring. He was out there all the time, watering, weeding, pruning, and keeping animals away. When he noticed they weren't growing as fast as he thought they should, he fertilized the soil; when that didn't encourage them, he sprinkled eggshells on the ground; when that didn't work, he watered them more. The tomato plants ended up dying, we didn't even see one tomato. He loved them to death.

"You have to plant the seeds and nurture the garden, and then at some point you need to sit back and let the plants grow." – Don Miguel Ruiz, *The Four Agreements*

If you're a perfectionist, surrendering will take practice, because it's against your nature to release control. When you release your need to go it alone, though, you benefit from a magnificent power that's there to support you. Next time you're rushing through your day, feeling like you have too much to do and not enough time to do it, take a moment to breathe deeply and say, "Everything is happening just the way it's supposed to." You will immediately let go and feel calmer. I do this in traffic all the time. If there's a slow driver in the left lane on the highway, and I start to get annoyed, I tell myself, everything is happening just the way it's supposed to; maybe this person is saving me from an accident up ahead. I immediately feel a shift in my energy.

Allowing doesn't have to be in opposition to achieving. In fact, if done correctly, it's a way to achieve at a higher level without burning your-self out. When you focus on achievement only, you can have a desperate energy come up, an energy that can work against you and that can drive people away.

This was about to happen to my client Sammy, who was responsible for business development at a large insurance firm. She called me freaking out one day because a warm prospect had ghosted her. She was worried that she had done something wrong to turn the prospect off. I reminded her that she was focusing on things that were out of her control. For example, she had no control over the timeline of this decision or on the prospect's competing priorities. The only things Sammy could control were her thoughts and her actions: how often she reached out to the prospect, and what she did to add value. I asked her how many other warm prospects she had in her pipeline, and she said one. That was a clear indication that she had all her eggs in one basket, which was making her feel a lot of pressure to make this deal. Sammy admitted that she wasn't comfortable networking, so she spent too much time on busywork. She needed to spend her time on actions that would lead to results, so I gave her an assignment to do the thing that made her feel the most uncomfortable, to spend the first hour of each day reaching out to quality prospects. After 12 weeks, she had scheduled more than 10 warm prospect meetings. By taking focused action every day, she was achieving better results, which gave her the confidence to let go of the outcome. Her energy had shifted from worried and frantic to confident and relaxed.

When you surrender, you're more intentional about the actions you take, and potentially more consistent. You put the work in because that's still important, then once you've done all you can do, detach from the outcome, and allow the universe to help you. It's all about energy – when you hold something too tightly, you end up driving it away; when you relax and have faith, you attract people and opportunities to you.

It can be upsetting when things don't go exactly as you planned, but there's often something bigger and better waiting around the corner. It's important to be open to what God or the universe has in store for you. If you're not comfortable listening to the universe, at the very least, listen to what your body is telling you. Have you ever made a decision and instantly felt tightness in your chest and a pit in your stomach? That's your body telling you something's wrong. I believe we're all born with specific gifts. When we use our gifts to help ourselves and to serve the greater good, we feel like we're in flow, (that's the feeling you get when time flies by). When we do something that takes us away from our gifts, we feel constricted, tight, heavy, or uneasy.

You have a sophisticated personal GPS system that's there to tell you what to do and where to go. Once you practice listening to it, it will guide you to places you've never dreamed of.

Practice Mindfulness

I'm writing this final chapter at a time when people are more stressed out than ever. The American Psychological Association recently published the results of its "Stress in America" survey, which shows that more than 80% of Americans feel stressed because of rising inflation, supply chain issues, and global uncertainty.[20] I would be willing to bet you've felt stressed out at some point in the last week or two. Stress sucks your energy and your time, keeping you focused on the future and what *could* happen. It makes you less effective and more unsure of yourself, and it keeps you from living your best life. You weren't meant to live that way.

Stress and anxiety come from fear, the fear that we won't be able to pay our bills, that things won't go our way, or that something bad will happen. When I tell my clients that, they always flinch and say, "I'm not scared, I'm just a little stressed." The word fear makes them uncomfortable, but once they realize it's a natural response to uncertainty and that everyone feels this way at some point, they let their guard down.

As soon as something happens that threatens our feeling of security, our mind searches for ways to take control, it scans all the likely scenarios, thinking it can mitigate a negative event by worrying about it. When our worries get the best of us, we create elaborate stories in our head that rarely come true. This cycle of vigilant overthinking is another way to be hard on ourselves because it doesn't allow us to relax and appreciate our blessings. We end up focusing on lack (all the possible negative scenarios) instead of abundance (the good things we already have in our lives).

One way to feel more compassion for yourself is to be present in the moment by practicing mindfulness. Lots of people I coach think mindfulness means meditation. Meditation is an amazing tool to become more consciously aware, but mindfulness is much more than that. It's about slowing down and paying attention to all the beautiful things in front of you and being present with the people you love. It's about listening to your heart and body and being honest with yourself about what's causing you pain. It's about taking time each day to focus on what you're grateful for, instead of spending mindless hours scrolling social media feeds that only make you feel bad about yourself.

At the beginning of every year, I think of all the topics that interest me and choose the one that calls out to me the most to focus on for the next 12 months. I research the topic by taking a course and reading a book or two a month on the subject. Last year, I chose ancient Eastern philosophies and religions. I've always been intrigued by Buddhism, but I wanted to deepen my understanding and commit to a more consistent meditation practice. I've meditated and prayed for years, but meditating was making me feel even more stressed out because I judged myself about how "well" I did it.

My research taught me that meditation is not about emptying your mind but about showing up over and over and simply allowing. Allowing thoughts to come up and then letting them go without judging them. Yeah right! I judged everything, especially myself. Another thing I struggled with was when the meditation experts said, pay attention to your breathing, but don't try to control it. That's like when someone tells you, "Don't look behind you!" Where's the first place you look? Behind you, of course. As soon as I pay attention to my breathing, I realize I've been holding my breath, so I take full, deep breaths. When I try to stop controlling it, my breath feels shallow again, so I breathe deeper, and so on. It took years for me to just let go. I slowly became more comfortable witnessing what was happening without being attached to it. I still like to breathe deeply when I meditate, but I don't worry about it so much anymore.

One of the most fundamental teachings of Buddhism is the recognition that where you are at this moment is exactly where you are meant to be, even if you don't like this moment. The most challenging realization for me was that suffering is an inevitable part of life. I will even go so far as to say it's necessary to live a full life. Think about it, if you felt happy all the time, it would become the status quo because there would be nothing to compare it to. To really appreciate the good things, you must experience some amount of suffering. That's what leads to growth. But there is a way to suffer less, and it starts with mindfulness.

Buddhist philosophy is based on The Four Noble Truths:[21]

Life is suffering.

Desire causes suffering.

It is possible to end desire.

The way to end desire is the eightfold path: right view, right intention, right speech, right action, right livelihood, right effort, right mindfulness, and right concentration.

Do you feel like you can't enjoy the moment because you're always focused on the next thing, then when you get to that next thing, the same thing happens, like a never-ending merry-go-round? Not being able to enjoy the moment is a form of suffering because it comes from your desire to be somewhere else. The only way out of it is to consciously shift your focus to what's happening right now. To breathe deeply and pay attention to what you're doing in this moment. Life is too precious to waste by wishing you were somewhere else most of the time. You are where you are, so how can you find joy in that?

In my research the word joy came up a lot. It made me ask myself this question: When's the last time I felt pure joy? I racked my brain and besides my kids being born, I couldn't come up with a time. There were times I felt content, but pure joy? I came up blank. I decided to make a conscious effort to feel more joy in my life. At first it felt forced, but the more I practiced, the more I realized it's possible. I also learned that joy can be a feeling that comes over you like a warm blanket on a cold night. It doesn't have to be a big, bold emotion, it can feel peaceful and nurturing.

This exercise taught me that you can choose your emotions at any given moment. When someone cuts you off in traffic, instead of getting annoyed, you can let it go. If you're stuck in a line at the supermarket, you can get frustrated, or you can take a moment to breathe or listen to your favorite podcast.

Our life on this earth is finite, and it goes by much quicker than we think it will when we're young. We spend so much of our precious time lost in our thoughts, either regretting things we said or did in the past or worrying about what may happen in the future.

"The past is already gone; the future is not yet here. There is only one moment for you to live, and that is the present moment." Buddha

I could tell you to stop thinking so much and just live in the moment, but I know from experience it's not that easy. It takes conscious effort, and it takes practice.

Next time you feel anxious, become consciously aware of the present moment by paying attention to what's going on in your body. This will help you connect with your heart. Your heart knows what's best for you, it's where your intuition comes from. When you push your emotions down, you're ignoring what your heart is trying to tell you and you get a constricting sensation in your chest. That's because your reality doesn't match up with what your soul wants. Fear keeps you from listening to the messages you get from your heart. The way to overcome this fear and pain is to learn to connect with your heart every day.

Here's a technique my clients and I use to release stress and anxiety:

You can do this sitting or lying down. I recommend doing it several times a day if you're feeling particularly stressed. Close your eyes and put your hands on your heart. Take a moment to feel it beating. Breathe deeply for three minutes, paying attention to your heart beating. Focus on the area around your heart and breathe into that area. If you feel thoughts come up, don't fight them, or try to force them out, just focus on your breathing and on your heart and they'll pass. Then, still focusing on your heart, think of something you're grateful for while you breathe. You can stay for longer than three minutes if you would like.

Take time throughout the day to breathe. You may have to do it again and again and that's OK. This will help you center yourself and clear your mind. You can shift your energy from tense to relaxed in minutes by simply breathing. When you notice yourself lost in thought, you can tell yourself, "I am in this moment," or "I'm here now." You can practice mindfulness anytime throughout the day, when you're walking, spending time with your kids or washing the dishes. A technique I learned that helped me find joy in the mundane is to think about the reason behind what I'm doing. For example, now when I fold the laundry, I think to myself, "This is a way for me to care for my family and to show them love." Sometimes I even find it relaxing. Don't judge me! I'm channeling Marie Kondo.

Another technique I use to appreciate the moment, is to think, *If I died tomorrow, how would my perception change about what I'm doing right now?* I know it's morbid, but it works every time to get me to appreciate every little moment. My energy shifts immediately, and I can let go of the stuff that doesn't matter. It also helps me focus on what's important, and to waste less time worrying about what might happen. Try it.

Manage Your Energy, Not Your Time

Have you ever had a day where you felt clear-headed and energized, like you could take on the world? A day when you completed your work with ease and ideas came to you effortlessly. Wouldn't it be great to feel like that every day? We all have moments or even days of high, positive energy but that feeling can be elusive, it seems to come out of nowhere, then it's gone before we realize it. The good news is we don't have to be at the mercy of our moods. Instead, we can take an active approach to maximizing our vitality every day by consciously focusing on the way we spend and replenish our energy.

Most of us don't allow ourselves the time we need to renew our energy. We keep our heads down for hours at a time, grinding through our work. Some of us started working at a time when that's what was required of us. We were rewarded for coming in early and leaving late, but that's an antiquated approach to work. Others put unnecessary pressure on themselves to push past their limits because they're uncomfortable setting boundaries or saying no. They pack too much into each day and end up feeling frustrated and depleted. They can get away with that for a while, but sooner or later, it takes a toll on their relationships and their well-being.

When your energy level is consistently taxed, you're more likely to lose patience and make mistakes, which can trigger your Drama Cycle. Living like that doesn't feel good, it creates a feeling of perpetual frustration and urgency, and can impact your health long-term.

In their book, *The Power of Full Engagement*, Jim Loehr and Tony Schwartz speak eloquently about the importance of intermittent energy renewal for optimal performance. They state that "energy, not time, is the fundamental currency of high performance, (and) the richest, happiest, and most productive lives are characterized by the ability to fully engage in the challenge at hand, but also to dis-engage periodically and seek renewal." Loehr, a performance psychologist, explains how he discovered the importance of intermittent energy renewal by observing elite tennis players to identify what set the best apart from the rest.

"I spent hundreds of hours watching players and studying tapes of their matches. To my growing frustration, I could detect almost no significant differences in their competitive habits during points. It was only when I began to notice what they did between points that I suddenly saw a difference. While most of them were not aware of it, the best players had each built almost exactly the same set of routines between points, these included the way they

walked back to the baseline after a point, how they held their heads and their shoulders, where they focused their eyes, the pattern of their breathing, and even the way they talked to themselves. It dawned on me that these players were instinctively using the time between points to maximize their recovery. Many lower ranked competitors I began to see had no recovery routines at all. When I hooked up the players to EKG telemetry, which allowed me to monitor their heart rates, I made another startling discovery, in the sixteen to twenty seconds between points in a match, the heart rates of top competitors dropped as much as twenty beats. By building highly efficient, and focused recovery routines, these players had found a way to derive extraordinary energy renewal in a very short period of time. Because lesser competitors had no comparable routines between points, their heart rates often remained at very high levels throughout their matches regardless of their level of fitness. The best competitors were using rituals to recover more efficiently and to better prepare for each upcoming point."[22]

Many of my clients tell me they understand the importance of rituals, but they don't have time to schedule one more thing into their day. I tell them that that's a limiting belief, and if they can't find fifteen minutes to spare, then there's probably something else they're not addressing. They may be hesitant to delegate, or they're uncomfortable setting boundaries or saying no. Or they could be wasting time doing things that feel good in the moment but aren't important. When we dig a little, we usually find some old, limiting people-pleasing pattern that needs to be addressed.

The most successful and productive people understand the power of energy. They take advantage of their natural energy cycles, and they schedule time to do things that renew their physical and mental energy.

"The greatest geniuses sometimes accomplish more when they work less."

—Leonardo DaVinci

Have you ever walked away from a full day of work feeling like you hardly got anything accomplished? Maybe you had a hard time concentrating, or you were so overwhelmed that you didn't know where to start.

That used to happen to me a lot. I wasted countless hours trying to force myself to focus, even when I felt depleted. After a while, I got burnt out. While writing this book, I noticed that I got more quality writing done in one hour early in the morning than in four hours in the afternoon. That's because creativity requires a high level of mental energy and focus. When I learned to do my most creative task at a time where my energy was naturally highest, I became more productive and less stressed.

If you want to maximize your energy, you may have to shift your mindset about productivity. You will need to give yourself permission to disengage from work, because your mind functions best when it's given time to recover. If the thought of taking time for yourself makes you uncomfortable, you may have some work to do to uncover your limiting beliefs. Focus on working, smarter, not harder, by practicing the steps in the exercise below for the next two weeks.

EXERCISE: Maximize Your Productivity and Vitality

For the next two weeks, schedule one uninterrupted hour a day, at least five days a week when your energy is at its highest, to work on your most challenging task. This task should require strategic thinking and/or creativity.

Schedule at least one, but preferably two, 15–30-minute breaks in your workday to do something that replenishes your mental energy. You can choose something from the list below or something you like to do that's not on this list.

Note: Do not use electronics or scroll social media during your breaks as they will not help you consciously renew your energy.

Activities to Renew Your Mental Energy for Your 15-30 Minute Breaks

Walk outside

Stretch/yoga

Read for pleasure

Take a nap (my favorite)

Spend time in nature

Meditate

Exercise

Take shower/bath .

Daydream

Play with a pet

Call a friend (not someone who drains your energy)

Draw

Journal

Dance

Sing

Listen to your favorite music or podcast

You Deserve Love

"If you want the moon, do not hide at night.

If you want a rose, do not run from the thorns.

If you want love, do not hide from yourself."

—Rumi

To have the kind of life you deserve, you must learn to love yourself as much as you love the people that are most precious to you, and you must stop feeling guilty about taking time for yourself. That means prioritizing your mental, physical, and spiritual well-being. When you give yourself the care you need, it keeps you out of the Drama Cycle because it helps you put things in perspective. You're better able to see things clearly and less likely to get triggered by other people. Conversely, when your energy is depleted, or you're tired, hungry, or overworked, small things can trigger your Drama Mode.

Taking time to balance your needs with your responsibilities will help you to be present for yourself and for the people in your life. It will not only help you to feel more confident and clear-headed, but it will also give you more patience and positive influence with others.

It may take consistent effort for you to remember to be kind to yourself, but that's OK. As long as you're committed to continue on the path of self-growth and fulfillment, it doesn't matter how many times you fall. When you're willing to get up again and again, and you have faith that there's a bigger plan in store for you, miraculous things will happen.

Summary

My wish for you is to free yourself from the stress that's been keeping you from living the life you're meant to live. To focus on what's most important to you every day and to find joy in the little things. To truly be yourself and stop caring so much about what people think about you.

If you've done the exercises in this book, you've learned something about the patterns that have been limiting you and causing you pain. You've also become aware of what makes you unique. You know that all human beings have strengths and weaknesses, and everyone suffers from fear and insecurities sometimes. You've learned how to lighten up and stop taking yourself so seriously, so you can love yourself as you are.

Personal growth is a lifelong journey. Whether this book is your first or ten thousandth step on that journey, you're right where you need to be. This is your opportunity to grow. Everything you've done up until now has led you here. You have a choice about what path you will take moving forward. You're being called to do great things.

Will you answer that call?

With gratitude and love,

Amal

One Page Review:

This page can be found at www.grammasexecutivecoaching.com. Download, print and display to take your first step toward feeling happier and more cofident

GRAMMAS COACHING

I KNOW YOU'RE IN THERE SOMEWHERE

ELEVATE YOUR MINDSET TO RELEASE STRESS & UNLOCK YOUR TRUE POTENTIAL

1 WHAT DO YOUR REALLY WANT?
- What must happen in the next 12 months for you to feel truly happy?
- Why is it a must?

2 HOW DO YOU WANT TO FEEL?
- What's your goal for self-growth?
- What's getting in your way?

3 WHAT'S YOUR #1 BLINDSPOT?
- What are people afraid to tell you about yourself?
- Which of the three needs is driving your blind spot?

4 WHAT ARE YOUR MANTRAS?
- What negative phrases do you repeat to yourself?
- How do they hurt you?

5 WHERE DID YOUR MAP COME FROM?
- Is there something from your past that's causing you pain?
- Are you ready to release it?

6 WHAT'S YOUR DRAMA MODE™?
- What are your three emotions under pressure?
- What's your Drama Mode™ called?

7 WHAT TRIGGERS YOU?
- What triggers your Drama Cycle™?
- How does it feel in your body?

8 WHAT'S YOUR POWER PERSONA™?
- What are the three emotions you want to feel?
- What's your Power Persona™ called?

9 HOW WILL YOU SHIFT YOUR STATE?
- What will you do to shift your energy when you're triggered?
- What will your new mantra be?

10 HOW DO YOU MEET YOUR NEEDS?
- How do you meet your need to feel connected, safe & worthy?
- Do you need to change the way you meet your needs?

11 WHAT WILL YOU FOCUS ON?
- What will you focus on when someone else behaves badly?
- How will you serve something bigger than yourself?

12 HOW WILL YOU FEEL YOUR BEST?
- What time will you work on your most challenging task each day?
- How will you replenish your energy?

Download for free at
www.grammasexecutivecoaching.com/free-resources

SOME OF MY FAVORITE BOOKS

Personal Growth/Spiritual/Inspirational

The Book of Joy, His Holiness the Dalai Lama, Archbishop Desmond Tutu

The Art of Happiness, His Holiness the Dalai Lama

Four Noble Truths, The Dalai Lama

Man's Search for Meaning, Viktor E. Frankl

The Go-Giver, Bob Burg, John David Mann

Loving What Is: Four Questions That Can Change Your Life, Byron Katie

As A Man Thinketh, James Allen

The Universe Has Your Back, Gabrielle Bernstein

Dying To Be Me, Anita Moorjani

29 Gifts, Cami Walker

I'm Spiritual, Dammit!, Jenniffer Weigel

This Isn't the Life I Ordered, Jenniffer Weigel

You Are Here, Thich Nhat Hanh

The Untethered Soul, Michael A. Singer

When God Becomes Real, Brian Johnson

A Return to Love, Marianne Williamson

Think Like a Monk, Jay Shetty

Many Lives, Many Masters, Brian L. Weiss, M.D.

Trauma

The Body Keeps the Score, Bessel A. van der Kolk

Happy Days, Gabrielle Bernstein

Leadership/Strategic Thinking

The Five Dysfunctions of a Team, Patrick Lencioni

Getting Naked, Patrick Lencioni

The Power of Full Engagement, Jim Loehr, Tony Schwartz

Crucial Conversations, Kerry Patterson

You Can't Send a Duck to Eagle School, Mac Anderson

Strategic Intuition, Bill Duggan

How to Think Like Leonardo da Vinci, Michael J. Gelb

Let Them Lead, John U. Bacon

Start with Why, Simon Sinek

The 7 Habits of Highly Effective People, Stephen R. Covey

Motivational

Think and Grow Rich, Napoleon Hill

Miracle Morning, Hal Elrod

Pound the Stone, Joshua Medcalf

The 5 Second Rule, Mel Robbins

Can't Hurt Me, David Goggins

Tuesdays with Morrie, Mitch Albom

ACKNOWLEDGEMENTS

It took three years and lots of help to complete this book. I am so grateful for the guidance, love, support, and editing help I received along the way. Thank you to Jenifer Frank, Charlene Jaszewski, Shirley Kalogeropoulos, Maggie Key, Bobby Manley, Pattie Manning, Joe Moran, Betsy Mulvey, Ashley Ryall, Yusuf Toropov, Lauren Wells, Ilham Yacteen, & Mia Yacteen.

I can't even begin to tell you how much I appreciate my clients, who choose to make personal growth a priority every day. You know who you are! You inspire me beyond measure to face the challenges of life with grace and love. Most importantly, thank you to Jimmy, Zoe & Yianni for listening to "just one more paragraph," and for loving me unconditionally.

ABOUT THE AUTHOR

Author, and Host of Grammas Leadership Podcast, Amal is a dynamic leadership coach and speaker with a direct, yet compassionate, approach. She's passionate about creating safe spaces for people to openly discuss the things we all go through but are afraid to talk about. As President of Grammas Executive Coaching, she works with leaders and entrepreneurs from a variety of industries, using her extensive background in personal development, business, and sales to help them take the steps needed to reach their highest potential.

Amal leads live events and online courses with individuals and organizations so they can shift their mindsets to feel more confident, motivated, and inspired. Visit www.grammasexecutivecoaching.com for more information.

NOTES

1. Doidge, Norman, M.D., *The Brain That Changes Itself: Stories of Personal Triumph from the Frontiers of Brain Science*, (Penguin, 2007). As referred to by Dr. Michael Merzenich, PhD, in *Soft-Wired: How the New Science of Brain Plasticity Can Change Your Life* (San Francisco, Parnassus Publishing, 2013).

2. Anders Ericsson and Robert Pool, *Peak: Secrets from the New Science of Expertise* (Boston: Houghton Mifflin Harcourt, 2016).

3. René A. Spitz, M.D., *Hospitalism, The Psychoanalytic Study of the Child, 2:1, 113-117* DOI: 10.1080/00797308.1946.11823540 (1946).

4. James S. House, Karl Landis, and Debra Umberson, "Social Relationships and Health," *Science* Vol. 265, 4865 (July 1988) DOI:10.1126/science.3399889.

5. Lieberman, Matthew D., *Social: Why Our Brains Are Wired to Connect* (New York, Crown Publishers, 2013).

6. Brooks, Arthur C., *Strength to Strength: Finding Success, Happiness, and Deep Purpose in the Second Half of Life*, (Portfolio/Penguin, 2022).

7. Williamson, Marianne, *A Return to Love: Reflections on the Principles of 'A Course in Miracles'* (New York, HarperCollins Publishers, 1992).

8. "The Last Dance," (sports documentary miniseries) ESPN Films and Netflix, directed by Jason Hehir, 2020. *https://www.netflix.com/title/80203144*

9. Mehrabian, Albert, *Nonverbal Communication* (New York, Routledge, 2017).

10. Jung, Carl G., *Psychology and Religion, West and East*, Vol. 11 (Princeton, New Jersey, Princeton University Press, 1958).

11. Von Franz, M.-L., "The Process of Individuation: The Realization of the Shadow," Chapter III, *Man and His Symbols*, Jung, Carl G. (Dell, 1968).

12. Amy Cuddy, "Your Body Language May Shape Who You Are," TEDGlobal, 2013, https://www.youtube.com/watch?v=Ks-_Mh1QhMc

13. Weigel, Jenniffer, *This Isn't the Life I Ordered* (Waterfront Press, 2015).

14. Burg, Bob and Mann, John David, *The Go-Giver: A Little Story About a Powerful Business Idea* (New York, Portfolio/Penguin, 2007 and 2015).

15. Inc. (Nov. 4, 2018 and updated Aug. 8, 2021), https://moneyinc.com/coffee-business-dutch-bros/

16. Beth Ewen, After IPO, Dutch Bros Chairman Says Brand Is 'Defying the Odds', Franchise Times, (Dec. 28, 2021) After IPO, Dutch Bros Chairman Says Brand Is 'Defying the Odds' | Franchise Insights | franchisetimes.com

17. Kaitlin Barbour, "Committed to a Culture: A Conversation with Travis Boersma, Founder and CEO of Dutch Bros Coffee," March 20, 2018, https://www.bbh.com/us/en/insights/private-banking-insights/committed-to-culture-a-conversation-with-travis-boersma-founder-.html

18. Erica R. Hendry, "7 Epic Fails Brought to You by the Genius Mind of Thomas Edison," *Smithsonian Magazine* (Nov. 20, 2013) www.

smithsonianmag.com/innovation/7-epic-fails-brought-to-you-by-the-genius-mind-of-thomas-edison-180947786

19. Canfield, Jack, Hansen, Mark Victor Hansen, Amy Newmark, *Chicken Soup for the Soul*, (Chicken Soup for the Soul Publishing, 2013).

20. American Psychological Association, *Stress in America 2022* (October, 2022), APA's Stress in America™ surveys measure attitudes and perceptions of stress among the general public. *www.apa.org/news/press/releases/stress/*

21. The Dalai Lama, *The Four Noble Truths,* (Thorsons, 1998).

22. Jim Loehr and Tony Schwartz, *The Power of Full Engagement: Managing Energy, Not Time, Is the Key to High Performance and Personal Renewal* (New York, The Free Press, 2003).